PARENTING WITH THE END IN MIND

PARENTING WITH THE END IN MIND

Practical Guidance With Biblical Principles

Jayna Coppedge

Copyright © 2016 Jayna Coppedge
All rights reserved.

ISBN-13:9781523949731

ISBN-10:1523949732

Parenting with the End in Mind: Practical Guidance with Biblical Principles
by Jayna Coppedge
www.jaynac.com

Cover design by Steve Coppedge
Cover photo purchased from Photo by winnond. Published on 02 September 2015
Stock photo - Image ID: 100356091

Author photo by Amanda Coppedge, Siloam Springs, AR

Scripture quotations marked (NIV) are from The Holy Bible, New International Version, ® (NIV®) Copyright © 1973,1978, 1984 International Bible Society, Used by permission of Zondervan Bible Publishers.

Scripture quotations marked (ESV) are from The Holy Bible, English Standard Version® (ESV®) Copyright © 2001 by Crossway, a publishing ministry of Good News Publishers. All rights reserved. ESV Text Edition: 2011.

Scripture quotations marked (MSG) are from *The MESSAGE*, copyright © by Eugene H. Peterson, 1993, 1994, 1995.
Used by permission of NavPress Publishing Group.

Scripture quotations marked (TLB) *The Living Bible* copyright © 1971 by Tyndale House Foundation. Used by permission of Tyndale House Publishers Inc., Carol Stream, Illinois 60188. All rights reserved.

Acknowledgments

Thank you to my partner in parenting and everything else for thirty-four years, my husband Steve. I can't imagine my life without your support. Thank you for joining me in this book: proofing, designing, and making graphics. I have courage, because you have my back.

Thank you to my children, Laura and Tyler. You make parenting fun. Life is always better when you are around.

Thank you to the congregation of First Baptist Church, Tahlequah OK. Your influence on me and my family for almost thirty years is immeasurable. We have laughed, cried, worshiped, prayed, played, and ministered to one another as a family. We will continue to love one another, as together we serve our Savior, Jesus.

Table of Contents

Acknowledgments ·v
Introduction · ix

Part 1: The Basics · 1
Chapter 1   What is your goal? · 3
Chapter 2   Treat your child with respect. · · · · · · · · · · · · · · · 7
Chapter 3   Boundaries provide freedom. · · · · · · · · · · · · · · ·11
Chapter 4   Action, not anger, motivates. · · · · · · · · · · · · · · ·15
Chapter 5   A miserable child is a blessed child. · · · · · · · · · ·19
Chapter 6   Try one of these twenty discipline techniques. · · · · · · · · · ·21
Chapter 7   Use multiple discipline techniques at the same time. · · · · · · · · ·33

Part 2: Relational Parenting and Successful Procedures · · · · · · · · 37
Chapter 8   Relational parenting prioritizes the child's long term benefit. ·39
Chapter 9   Chores create capable adults. · · · · · · · · · · · · · · ·47
Chapter 10 Meal time as an example of parenting with respect. · · · · · · · · ·53
Chapter 11 Autopsy your parenting failures to discover warning signs. · · ·57
Chapter 12 Accept your child as made by God. · · · · · · · · · · · · ·63

Part 3- Pregnancy and The First Year · · · · · · · · · · · · · · · · · 73
Chapter 13 Parenting begins in the womb. · · · · · · · · · · · · · · · · ·75
Chapter 14 Begin parenting with the end in mind now. · · · · · · · · · · · ·79

Chapter 15 Enjoy the first year. ·83
Chapter 16 Parenting the first year made easier. ·87

    A Final Word· ·91
    About the Author ·93

Introduction

"With all the parenting books on the market and with all the Christian childrearing books on the reduced price shelves, why are you spending months writing another one?" I asked myself. I laid this book aside several times because the process just seemed impossible. When I shared these principles in a parenting class in the fall of 2015, the audience looked at me as if I was an oasis in a desert. I was obviously providing hope. Almost every week new couples joined and they took extra copies of the handouts to share with friends. So I wrote this book; it is written from the material I shared with parents for over two decades.

Most parents are so overwhelmed with the here and now that they forget they are raising an adult. Because these parents do not have a vision of who their child is to become, their child enters adulthood ill prepared for life. Parenting with the end in mind means knowing the skills your child must master. Your ultimate goal guides your daily decisions.

As a children's minister, for twenty-four years I have a longitudinal perspective of entire family systems that makes this book different. I walked with the same children and parents from potty training, through sibling rivalry, peer issues, and most importantly the development of their faith. As a surrogate parent, I played with, taught, and slept in the room with these children at camp, on mission trips, and slumber parties. I prayed for, prayed with, and observed hundreds of children, all the while learning from child specialists at conferences.

Even after my two children were raised and I retired, I find myself studying child development. Forty years ago God developed in me an interest in understanding people that has not dissipated. This book shares the most key elements of raising children, I found in all of my research and experience.

I hope this book is very practical and the descriptions resonate with you. I provide the "why" as well as the "what to do." Finding a balance between too strict and too lenient, too complacent and too involved is very different in each circumstance. Every parent must seek God's guidance to adapt any philosophy to his or her uniquely designed child. Often I wanted to add my phone number so I could make the example fit your child's temperament.

Please remember, I am not a doctor so do not substitute my opinions for the advice of professionals. I am sharing what I have learned, knowing that not all advice is appropriate for every situation.

Your powerful influence to crush or empower your child's spirit should force you to your knees in prayer. Raising him or her to be the person God designed, guiding him or her to transfer his or her dependence from you to the Lord is thrilling, hair raising, and frustrating. Thank you for letting me join your adventure.

3 John 4,

Jayna Coppedge

Part 1: The Basics

1

What is your goal?

Parenting with the end in mind means taking the time to visualize the person who you hope your child will become. What is your heart's desire for your child at age twenty-two? Describe his character, his values, his attitude, and his heart. It will take years before you will see the results of your effort. Regardless of what you do, he will get older; but if you delay, your goal will not be achieved. Childrearing cannot be postponed.

Of course, your child will reflect your heart. If your integrity is lacking, do not expect him to respect you. If you are living on credit, how will you teach self-discipline? It is not too late for you to change. Watching your transformation will give him the courage to do the hard work of growing into a responsible adult. Notice, I did not ask you to describe his vocation. Your duty is to follow God's plan:

> *"Hear, O Israel: The LORD our God, the LORD is one. Love the LORD your God with all your heart and with all your soul and with all your strength. These commandments that I give you today are to be on your hearts. Impress them on your children. Talk about them when you sit at home and when you walk along the road, when you lie down and when you get up. Tie them as symbols on your hands and bind them on your foreheads. Write them on the door frames of your houses and on your gates." (Deuteronomy 6:4-9 NIV)*

> **Parenting Goals:**
> Christ-follower
> Honest
> Diligent
> Loyal
> Godly
> Active in church
> Financially responsible
> Self-sacrificing
> Loving
> Perseveres
> Prays
> Many good friends
> Reads Bible
> Joyful
> Respectful
> Courageous

God didn't write, "Teach your child to be an accountant or a missionary." He says, "Impress them to love Him, and follow His commandments." He doesn't advise, "Do everything to make your children happy, fulfilled, or live a life of luxury." If he delights in God, contentment will result.

> *Take delight in the Lord, and he will give you the desires of your heart. (Psalms 37:4 NIV)*

Society does not suggest anyone's purpose is to give God glory. Rather it encourages us to live vicariously through our children. Satan whispers, "Entertain, indulge, they are children for such a short time." Solomon contrasts by showing that knowing you have done your job well gives true contentment.

> *"That each of them may eat and drink, and find satisfaction in all their toil—this is the gift of God." (Ecclesiastes 3:13 NIV)*

Use your vision as a guide for your daily decisions. Make the decision that brings that future picture into focus. When deciding between encouraging her to do the school homework project, or giving the teacher a tongue-lashing for creating this time-consuming assignment, which do I choose? Aim for the one that imparts perseverance even when life doesn't make sense.

> *"If anyone forces you to go one mile, go with them two miles." (Matthew 5:41 NIV)*

If you discover that by allowing your daughter to play in a traveling sports team she will miss Sunday worship thirteen times, you say "God is more important than sports; God will give you other opportunities to develop your talent without sacrificing worship services."

What is your goal?

"Bear in mind that the Lord has given you the Sabbath; that is why on the sixth day he gives you bread for two days. Everyone is to stay where they are on the seventh day; no one is to go out. So the people rested on the seventh day." (Exodus 16:29, 30 NIV)

Parenting with the end in mind is noticing a trend in your son that is counterproductive to your goal. It is not only punishing disobedience; it is steering him into the best habits. For example, if he is often shouting, "I can't find it anywhere." Rather than asking the same questions, like: "Did you look...?" and "Where was it last?" Create a finder's fee. Ask how much are you willing to pay someone to find this? The goal is not to make family members start charging one another, the goal is to make the person who keeps loosing things to stop expecting everyone to rescue them. I paid five dollars to the child who found my car keys. I once earned a dollar for a lost shoe. Communicate through action that time is money, "We are not going to help you search for items lost in your dorm room."

Wanting your child to be courteous and loyal, you avoid trash talking about others.

"The tongue has the power of life and death" (Proverbs 18:21 NIV)

Believing in the power of prayer, you ask for God's guidance before purchasing your car, choosing a doctor, and starting your day. Yes, it is true you can make all the right decisions and your child may refuse to develop godly character; everyone does have free will. However, how many times have you done or said something just like your parents even though you promised yourself you wouldn't?

"I have set you an example that you should do as I have done for you." (John 13:15 NIV)

When you know your goal, it is much easier to make the best, though not easiest, choices for your family. Remember your priorities will probably become hers. She will most likely imitate you.

"Each of you should use whatever gift you have received to serve others, as faithful stewards of God's grace in its various forms. If anyone speaks, they should do so as one who speaks the very words of God. If anyone serves, they should do so with the strength God provides, so that in all things God may be praised through Jesus Christ. To him be the glory and the power for ever and ever. Amen." (1 Peter 4:10, 11 NIV)

2

Treat your child with respect.

I grew up being teased until I cried. This did not happen on the school grounds, but in my home. Being tickled until I wept hot tears of helpless anger was normal for me. People jumped out from behind doors all of my preschool years. My reaction was the family entertainment. Fifty years later, I still startle too easily.

If your parenting goal is to raise an adult with self-respect, then you begin treating her with respect when she is a preschooler. Using words of encouragement, recognizing that each person is important to the family, and expressing appreciation to one another can become the new routine. Choose an attitude of humble service to foster family unity and security. When members feel loved and accepted, they will easily laugh at themselves without being defensive.

Avoid insincerity such as sarcasm, flattery, negative nicknames, or cruel teasing as they are dishonest and selfish. Names such as "hurricane," "fraidy cat," "couch potato" will do nothing to improve family relationships regardless of their accuracy. Words lead to destiny. Treat your children with the respect deserved for God's unique creation.

> *"The words of the reckless pierce like swords, but the tongue of the wise brings healing." (Proverbs 12:18 NIV)*

While selfishness is a sin, self-respect is a virtue. When dignity is freely given then the atmosphere is not hostile. When we develop the common purpose to serve one another, everyone cleaning the house is the logical outcome. You will function like a small church with each one contributing the household.

> "If one member suffers, all suffer together; if one member is honored, all rejoice together." (1 Corinthians 12:26 ESV)

Seldom is rage expressed in a respectful manner, therefore parents must teach conflict resolution skills. If I am going to love my neighbor as I love myself, I must know how to handle disagreements. If someone does not feel safe in his family, it will be harder for him to trust other people.

Children who experience a parent's unconditional love are better able to surrender their lives to the all-knowing Savior. This does not mean parents should not have high expectations of their children. An element of fear is found in the reverence we have for the Lord. We recognize that God is the one with the power. God expects us to surrender our will and obey His commands. Just as it would be foolish to turn over the controls of an airplane to a person who has never flown, it is unloving to give children too much control over their lives without training them first. Children have a sin nature; modeling politeness is not enough to bring out their best. They must also fear the consequences of their actions.

> "He who fears the Lord has a secure fortress, and for his children it will be a refuge." (Proverbs 14:26 NIV)

Disrespectful behaviors include interrupting two people talking. When a parent is talking with someone else, a four-year-old can wait to speak until his parent acknowledges him. When he approaches touch him. Ignoring him is rude; he will misbehave, if necessary, to get your attention. Once the person speaking finishes their thought, then give him your attention. Waiting thirty seconds will seem like an eternity to him, but it is an important lesson.

> "A fool shows his annoyance at once, but a wise man listens to advice." (Proverbs 12:15 NIV)

Treat your child with respect.

Set the example of tidying your own belongings. Children do imitate what they see. When your spouse does not do what is requested, do not mutter under your breath, or nag, or complain; instead demonstrate serving with a joyful spirit.

> *"Better to live alone in a tumbledown shack than share a mansion with a nagging spouse."* (Proverbs 21:9 MSG)

The bottom line, treat your family members the way you would want to be treated. Forgive one another when feelings are hurt, stop any laughter or poking fun when malice is found. Remember that every person is created in God's image and Jesus loved him or her enough to die for him or her.

3

Boundaries provide freedom.

If you have traveled in countries without painted highway lines or guard rails, you know how frightening the traffic can be. Those simple yellow marks make you feel less exposed to the whimsy of an oncoming motorist. When there was a small barrier between me and the Grand Canyon, I walked right up to the edge to enjoy the view. When the there was no fence, I stayed yards away from the edge. I didn't want to take a chance on a rock coming loose or my stumbling.

Your rules give your son the courage to be curious and explore the world. When he knows that you will catch him, he will dive in the deep end of the pool. Your guidance gives him the security necessary for him to develop into the person God designed.

Imagine climbing to the top of a trapeze. Would you test the net to see if it was secure and could hold you if you fell? Would you quickly trust each rung of the ladder even once you were six stories high? How experienced would you need to be, until you quit double checking the bar when you grabbed it? It is the same with your toddler; he will keep stretching his time away from you as long as you are right where he left you.

Since we cannot be with our children all the time, we establish the boundaries as surrogate parents. These guidelines keep our children from harm, however they are as easily crossed as that yellow highway line. When

I teach the importance of boundaries I always draw the graphic below on the left hand side is very narrow. It represents the toddler years, when you limit her experience with stairwells and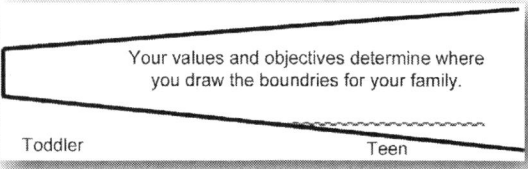
strangers. She has a very small amount of freedom. The other end shows adulthood when you no longer have any restraints over her. The dashed line represents the occasions when another authority figure has more stringent rules than you. There will be times when teachers, coaches, ministers or employers will have rules that you and your teen must obey.

The more responsible she is to stay within the rules, the broader the boundaries become. Her options grow as she stays within your guidelines. You are a teammate assisting her as she races to adulthood. You will do everything possible to assist in her quest to complete independence. She reaches age eighteen as a wise, self-disciplined, skilled woman of integrity.

You are also the referee. Just as in the game of basketball, if she steps out or bounds, the game will stop and a penalty will be given. When her performance stays within your range of what is acceptable, she can move unhindered. When she challenges your authority, then you must stop her progress and impose a "penalty" that reinforces the limit.

When my children were teens, I drew this diagram. I explained, "I don't want to blow the whistle anymore. I just want to stand back and cheer you on through graduation. But I love you too much to let you destroy your chance of success by ignoring a bad attitude or conduct. I will enforce the rules; if I don't, someone who doesn't love you will. If you respectfully explain to me why a rule is too restrictive, I will consider your opinion, and I may redraw the line. "

All children will test the limits to make sure that you are still protecting them. I remember specifically when my daughter was twenty to twenty-two months. There were days when every activity was a challenge. She ran from me when I tried to dress her, she closed her mouth when I offered food, she was establishing that she was a separate person from me. Knowing this was

Boundaries provide freedom.

happening, I let her decide between the red or blue shirt, and between the apple or the pear, but I was still the boss. She still had to take a nap, get dressed, ride in the car seat, and hold my hand in parking lots. Once she realized I was not going to change my mind about who was in charge, she became pleasant and compliant for weeks. Periodically, especially when a developmental milestone occurred she would again try to mutiny. All the while I was systematically giving her more responsibility and autonomy.

Without rules, there is no game. Every parent's job is to clearly define and enforce their family's values. If you do not establish strong boundaries, he will not grow as confident in his ability to handle life. He will be insecure, afraid to use his freedom, fearing he will stumble into the grand canyon of failure.

4

Action, not anger, motivates.

Many parents falsely believe that unless they get mad, their child will never obey. When my husband was a child he and his sister played all over the neighborhood until his mom called them in for supper. When his mom called "Steve! Teresa! Dinner!" they knew supper was almost ready. "Steven Walter, Teresa Lynn dinner!" meant about ten more minutes until they would have to stop and eat. The moment they heard her whistle, they ran home. They knew from painful experience that their time was up.

Since many parents do not take action against disobedience until they are upset, they believe it was the anger instead of the consequence that gets the results. Once a parent discovers great outcomes are possible without losing his or her temper, the entire atmosphere of their home is changed.

"You are trying my patience." "You are on my last nerve." "No more chances." These are all "blah blah blah," to a child. I don't know what I did this time, but I remember my dad saying, "I ought to spank you." I am grateful, I only rebelled in my mind, because I thought, "Yeah, but you are too old and lazy to do anything but talk." I had disdain for his words.

If you keep threatening instead of acting, you will lose your ability to think logically. Irate, you will yell the most ridiculous ineffective commands and chastisements. Frustrated, now you'll attack his spirit instead of dealing with the contrary behavior. Parents who take action before reaching their point of rage seldom succumb to physical or verbal abuse.

For example, you are at a family reunion and you want Sandy to play with her cousins. So even though she is acting sassy, you ignore it. However, she keeps pushing it, she is whiney, and refuses to share with her sister, and then she spills soda on herself. As the last straw, you lose most of your self-control. Sandy is confused because you are yelling at her over an accident. She does not realize that you are punishing her for all of her misdeeds of the day. All she can remember is the last offense. She doesn't respond with understanding and repentance from this discipline. She screams with emotional outrage at the unfairness of your reaction. She also feels insecure and frightened, because her mom is not acting normal. If you took her aside and dealt with her attitude and conduct sooner, you would not have embarrassed yourself, and when she spilled the soda, you had dealt with it without the emotion.

> **In most families you hear:** "As soon as that show is over, pick up your toys and go take a bath."
> **~5 minutes after the show is over:** "Your show is over, go take your bath."
> **~20 minutes after:** "John David, you better be in that tub!"
> **~30 minutes after:** Mom comes in screaming: "How many times do I have to tell you to get in the bathtub?" She starts throwing the toys in the container, she turns off the TV, she grabs him by the arm and marches him to the bathroom.

In the diagram above you see that the parent doesn't take action until she has reached wrath.

If you are not sure where your action line is, then ask someone around you when your parenting. Your child definitely knows. It is his number one priority to know. Steve and Teresa both knew, listen for the whistle.

In Action Driven Parenting you will gain compliance through involvement without any screaming or anger or threats.

Action, not anger, motivates.

> **Action Driven Parenting:** "As soon as that show is over, pick up your toys and go take a bath."
> **~1 minute after the show is over:** "Are you picking up?" If she is, no action needed. If she isn't, calmly turn off the TV, watch her pick up the toys, and escort her to the bathroom. When she asks to stay up and read, you reply: "I want to say yes, but you didn't pick up the toys promptly, maybe tomorrow night."
>
> Instructions Given — **Transition Adjustment** — 1 minute Follow Through  No Anger Needed

Try this: touch her shoulder and say, "Jenny, it is almost time for you to stop playing, pick up your dolls, and take a bath. When the buzzer goes off, there will be no 'in a few minutes.' If you want, you can start getting ready any time before the buzzer." If you have a very strong-willed child, she will be less defiant when you provide her with a choice. So she can choose to comply before the buzzer goes off. When you hear the buzzer call, "Jenny, tell me you heard the buzzer and you are obeying." If she responds, then after three minutes make sure she is following through. If she is picking up, you can give her a high five or say nothing. If she isn't, then calmly enforce a penalty.

Jenny may be baffled by your expectations of obedience. She may think that you weren't serious about taking a bath so soon. She thought that you did not really want her to take a bath until you had at least shouted her middle name. Your correction the first time may be a scolding with you watching to see that she follows through. The second failure to comply needs to be a consequence, plus a promise of a larger "reminder" if she "still can't remember to obey". It is critical that you are consistent, if you slip back into old habits, she will risk that her disobedience will be rewarded with more playtime.

Slot machines are so addictive because if there is a reward, it will be completely random. If you do not follow through on your threats or promises, you are programing your child to disregard your words. When you change your mind explain why say, "I just remembered that there's no school tomorrow so you can play thirty minutes later," or not be able to keep a promise, "I am really disappointed too, but Ashley cannot spend the night. Peter's cough could be contagious." When those occur, explain immediately why this is an exception.

The entire atmosphere of your home will change when you stop using anger to motivate. You can also eliminate yelling using the same methodology. She can be trained to listen to your natural speaking cheerful voice, by simply taking action before you yell.

God convicted me about the fact that I never yelled at the children at church and yet I was yelling at my children daily. "Kids, I must stop my bad habit of shouting at you. God told me that it was disrespectful. Since I don't scream at other people's kids and since I don't love them as much as I love you, I should stop yelling at you. Would you like to help me in this project?" I took complete responsibility for my behavior. I refused to blame them when I failed. "When you catch me yelling, I want you to put one finger on your lips to remind me. When you remind me, or I catch myself, I will apologize and I will slap my hand hard." I was surprised at how much it hurt my hand, and how quickly I changed. I taught myself to stop before getting to the boiling point. As an added bonus I modeled self-control for my children.

Your parental authority and the atmosphere of your home are all controlled by your willingness to take the appropriate action sooner rather than later.

5

A miserable child is a blessed child.

Yes, I do mean miserable; it is not a typo. A blessed girl is one who knows her parents love her too much not to make her miserable when she has disobeyed. A happy boy's parents refuse to buy him even small items, like a box of cereal if it is not good for him. Parents who try to be their daughter's best friend are foolish.

I know a child who responds to most things with an eye roll and an attitude, saying, "this is so lame". He is the unhappiest guy I know. Why is everything around him so stupid? Well, he had too many experiences at a much too young of an age, so most of life is "lame" in comparison.

I know this sounds radical, but occasionally the best parents are a little selfish. A family is not a democracy where everyone has a vote of equal standing; it is a benevolent dictatorship. Determine that you will do what is best for the whole family, regardless of how unhappy it may make a particular child on occasions. By allowing my children choices occasionally, we made these exceptions into events. A preschool child can only choose between two or three options. Therefore, do not give him the responsibility of choosing the family restaurant on a consistent basis. As a special occasion, she picks where to eat.

For infants, the world does literally revolve around them. Their needs are put above everything and everyone. Unfortunately, many parents get into this habit and do not make the transition into the season when the child must do the adapting to the world.

If your daughter is allowed to decide for the family, she gets the wrong message: I am more important than other people. She will express her wants as needs. You must distinguish the difference. Always meet her needs, but only occasionally give in to her wants.

When children own too many toys, they are less likely to enjoy their toys. Too many possibilities can be overwhelming, she may not be able to decide with what to play, or she may be distracted by the other toys. Therefore, she flits from shelf to floor, shortening her attention span.

Remember Veruca Salt in the book *Charley and The Chocolate Factory*? She was an insecure tyrant. Today it is so much easier to spoil children. We have so much more money, and so many opportunities. I believe often parents take their kids to events simply out of reflex. All of their Facebook friends took their children, so they didn't even consider not going. When I was a children's minister, children would tell me how much they enjoyed their Saturdays at home. Some parents' greatest fear is that their child might be bored.

Without misery, she is not prepared for the real world. Deceived, she thinks employers will make exceptions for her. The worst goal a parent can have is trying to keep a child happy. Children need to learn how to make themselves happy.

6

Try one of these twenty discipline techniques.

A discipline technique is an action taken to prevent a misdeed from happening. Causing the child to regret not obeying their parent and make a better choice in the future often requires a form of punishment. Not every child will respond to every method, nor should the same procedure be used for every misbehavior. For some children a snap of a finger and a stern look will be enough to get them to get back inside the boundaries at dinner time. She knows that if she continues, the consequence will be unpleasant enough that her current fun is not worth the price. If a parent is not consistent in following through with action, she may decide the fun is worth the gamble.

Ultimately the goal is for her to discover the joy in making good decisions. You want to raise an adult that does the right thing out of integrity, not because he is afraid of being caught, embarrassed, or reprimanded. No longer driven to please parents, she knows that she is happier when she follows the regulations of good citizenship.

1. **Redirection** (all ages) is moving him to a different activity, or location. When your toddler wants to play with the TV remote, you place a squeaky toy in one hand while removing the remote from the other hand. If your older child is turning cartwheels in front of the TV, say, "I think you have too much energy to play inside. I want you to go play outside for a while." This redirection prevents a problem from developing.

2. **Firm or painful touch** (use with young preschooler) is slapping his hand with a firm "No" is often enough to deter him from playing with the electrical cord. When you swat him on the diaper, it doesn't have to sting, as much as startle to get him to stop. Holding his hand, frowning, and saying no may convince him that pulling someone's hair is unacceptable.

   When one child hurts another one, always go to the victim first. It is important that your attention doesn't go to the misbehavior before empathy is expressed. This allows the aggressor to begin to feel regret. By giving your adrenaline a moment to subside, you are less likely to overreact. Ignoring attention seeking misconduct, because you are drying the victim's tears, serves as a deterrent from attacking another child. When you are ready to deal with the attack, use any of these techniques.

3. **Isolation** (2- 12 year-olds) is removing her from the rest of the group when she continues defy your instruction. She is sent to a boring, safe location for a set number of minutes for the purpose of changing her attitude and behavior. When God gave Jonah isolation in the belly of a fish, He didn't let Jonah out until he repented.

   Do not start timing the isolation until she is complying by sitting still and quiet. A child rebelling against the separation may need a spanking followed by isolation. When you return for her ask, "Are you ready to start sharing?" "Are you still going to throw balls in the house?" "What are you going to do differently?" "Is there something you need to say to Grandma?" During her thinking time, she needs to find a solution. Do not begin this process if you are not willing to spend the time needed to enforce it. For example, don't use it when you are late for an appointment.

4. **Time-out** (for all ages) is giving your child or yourself the time to regain perspective. While isolation is used as a punishment, time-out is a gift. The difference in practice is subtle, especially to a young child; therefore, you will convey isolation with a frown and tone. Use time-out when he is too energetic for his location, but not defiant or

Try one of these twenty discipline techniques.

disobedient. With an understanding, loving manner say, "Hey, buddy, let's relax a minute over here before you start getting on Grandpa's nerves." When he is younger, or when this is a new experience, stay with him to show that he is not in trouble.

Another way time-out is different, is that he determines how long the break is. He may stay away from the group for two minutes or he may decide to do something else.

"Time-out" is a great code word in a family. When you are feeling overwhelmed, you can declare "time-out" meaning everyone go away and leave me alone for a while. It communicates: I am going to my room, or for a walk, no one follow me. Teach your child that taking a break is a good option to regain perspective.

When children are wrestling and tickling with each other or a parent, anyone can say "time-out" to catch their breath without admitting defeat. Children need to be physical with one another, but they don't need to overpower others in defeat. This practice is respectful and prevents bullying. If the weakest child cries "time-out" too often, naturally the rest won't play with him, so he will get braver or not play.

5. **Shouting "No!"** (use when someone is about to be harmed). Shouting no will cause the child to pause for a moment. This gives you time to prevent the punch, the block from being thrown, the child from touching the stove, or the child running toward the street. This routine is only effective if it is rarely used. It will become white noise if you yell often. You may need to do more to make certain your child does not follow through with his intention.

6. **Reasoning** (use with 4-year-old or older) is explaining why you will not allow them to do something. Some children respond well to logic. "Never throw scissors, because when you do, the sharp end could injure someone." If she argues with your reasoning, then choose another procedure.

Although I often used biblical principles to explain my reasons, I only required my children to look up Bible verses or a Bible story a few times. I presented the experience not as punishment, but as an explanation. For example: *"not giving up meeting together, as some are in the habit of doing, but encouraging one another,"* (Hebrews 10:25 NIV) answered why we consistently attended church.

7. **Grounding, removal of a privilege** (all ages) is eliminating the toy that they are fighting over. Stopping a play date because of hitting, leaving a park because he wouldn't stay out of the water, or returning a package of gum to the store shelf are all logical consequences for a preschooler. When the result leads to a temper tantrum, stay strong, and add additional penalties.

    For an older child, it is a sentence for a longer period of time, so that he regrets his decision. Thinking before you choose how he will be grounded is critical. You may wait until the next day, so your verdict is rational or in harmony with the other parent. Often the anticipation can be worse than the penalty. Make sure you will follow through with your pronouncement. When you are specific, you will be less likely to need to make an exception. "You are grounded until your thirty," or "No media for a week;" are not well thought out. "You can't go to Karen's birthday party next month," means you are punishing Karen as well.

8. **Natural consequences** (every age) is allowing her to suffer from her decisions. Let the outcomes get her attention. DO NOT say, "I told you so." Say compassionately, "Aww that's too bad, or sorry to hear that." DO NOT lecture, or she will transfer her annoyance onto you. She needs to be frustrated with herself. Allow her to get too hot or cold from her clothing selection.

    If he argues over insect repellent, then hope, to yourself, he gets mosquito bites. Do not intervene when he can't buy popcorn because he bought the toy. Much later you can discuss a solution for next time. Try saying, "Would you like to come up with some ideas to avoid that same problem?" If he wants a suggestion, then be helpful. Perhaps he wants to figure out his own solution.

9. **Spanking** (for children 18 months to 6 years) is hitting a child's bottom with a stick, paddle, or flyswatter. Only spank your child when

he is willfully defying your authority, and milder measures failed. It will often improve a child's attitude. Do not spank if he is forgetful, or irresponsible. If he is acting dangerous to others or is being devious, a spanking may be helpful. For example, do not spank because she broke a dinner plate; however, if she hid the broken plate and lied about it, a spanking may be a reminder for her not to lie the next time.

A spanking is more formal than a slap on the hand or a swat on the behind to get your child's attention. Always spank her in private. It is demeaning to be disciplined in front of an audience. Never spank her when you are angry. It is too easy to spank too hard or too long. There is a very fine line between a hard spanking and child abuse. Determine how many strikes you will give before beginning. Three is usually adequate.

He should experience enough discomfort to change his rebelliousness. Make sure he understands the reason for the spanking before the pain. If he doesn't understand, you will plant seeds of resentment. If he slams doors, calls you names or stares you in the eye and says defiantly, "That didn't hurt," the spanking was ineffective. If that happens, a good strategy is to put him in isolation, so that both of you calm down while you decide how you can alter his attitude.

Do not withhold love following a spanking. Many children are embarrassed and want reassurance that all is forgiven. If he shows a soft heart following the spanking, then it accomplished its purpose.

10. **Extinction** (every age) is ignoring a problem when she is trying to manipulate you. This manipulation can come in the form of a temper tantrum, pouting, fake crying to get a sibling in trouble, heavy sighs, comparing a friend's parents to you, and any attempt to bait you into a power struggle. By ignoring the drama, you maintain all the power. You can incorporate a mantra if she is determined. "I am ignoring you until you speak with respect." You may also use isolation. "You may go to your room until…" It is critical that you do not reinforce this performance by giving into it.

11. **Mantras** (every age) are repeated phrases reminding him of your expectation. It also reminds you not to give into his misconduct. It is most effective if your voice has the same monotone, with no emotion. "Little girls cannot say no to their mothers," proved to be useful with my fourteen-month old daughter. She would tell me no while I put her to bed, gave her bath, or dressed her. She was trying to establish her independence. I reminded her, she had no power over me. I would repeat the mantra every time she told me no, eventually she would repeat the mantra to herself and gave up arguing. It took a while, but it was very effective.

    Mantras work really well with a whining or argumentative child. "I do not understand whining, come back and try again," or "With good manners please." Refuse to answer her question, or reply with anything other than the mantra, until she speaks properly. Occasionally you may have to reinforce your command by taking her by the hand and escorting her out of the room and shutting the door. If you lose your temper, she wins. Try out, "I will not be buying anything extra today." "I expect you to obey."

    Mantras have power; I used the following mantra for weeks to change my outlook. "1st Corinthians 13:4-7: I am patient, I am kind. I do not envy, I do not boast, I am not proud. I do not dishonor others, I am not self-seeking, I am not easily angered, I do not keep a record of wrongs. I do not delight in evil, instead I rejoice in the truth."

    When my daughter struggled putting on her shoes, or zipping her coat, she would become frustrated and burst into tears. I started, "I know this is hard, but you can do hard things." This is so powerful, because it doesn't discount the emotion, instead it encouraged her to try again. Occasionally I would include, "If you come over here, I will be your helper." This statement reinforces the idea that family helps one another.

    "I know this is hard, but you can do hard things," became our family moto: decades later, we often quote it to one another or ourselves. I know a few elementary school teachers who use this phrase in their classroom, and a family that has "This Family Does Hard Things" hanging on their wall.

12. **Logical Consequence** (4-year-old or older) is creating a result and requires the ability to see this is caused by their choice or conduct. The more logical or memorable the result, the more effective it will be. It is always better to have the ability to expand penalty, than having to reduce the consequence, because you started too extreme. "Since you forgot to bring in the tools and they got rusty, you must scrub the rust off." "Since you tracked mud on to the carpet a third time, in addition to scrubbing up the stain, you will be vacuuming the carpet every Saturday for the next three weeks. If you track mud again, then you will sweep off the porch as well for the next four weeks."

One of my favorite examples occurred when a 2nd grader kept pealing the vinyl off of his dining room chair. When he came into the kitchen for breakfast there was a sign, "Out of Order" taped to his chair. His mom casually explained, "That chair isn't useable because you picked the vinyl off." He asked, "Where am I going to sit?" Matter-of-factly she answered, "Hmm, I guess you will eat standing until it is repaired." It took three days for her to find time to buy the tape to fix the chair. His kindergarten brother was overheard saying, "Yeah, that is why I never tear-up my chair." His three-year-old sister concluded on her own that if she doesn't stay seated during meal time, she might lose her chair. I love this story, because I see these kids laughing when they are in college about the time Samuel's chair was out of order.

13. **Reinforcement** (every age) is encouraging her when she is behaving. Word your comment so that she notices how happy she is about her choice. "I know you are proud of yourself; good job not yelling back at your sister." "Wow, I know you wanted to give up, but you didn't look at what you accomplished." Reinforce not only the behavior, but her sense of self satisfaction. If you use this method more often than once a week, or if you start becoming predictable so that she expects it, then it loses its effectiveness.

14. **Meet physical needs** (every age) by giving him food, or a nap. An observant parent senses what he needs before he becomes cranky or disobedient. Treat him the way you would want to be treated. Do not have unrealistic expectations or set him up for failure.

    Although will you lower your expectations when she is ill, do not remove your boundaries all together. When parents remove the rules, she will feel less secure, and more frightened. It is hard at times for parents to maintain their standards for a child with a chronic illness; however, siblings and the ill child will suffer additionally, if too many exceptions are made.

15. **Meet emotional needs** (every age) by recognizing that he needs to know you love him. Remember the story of the babies in the orphanage during the WWII who were fed, and had all their physical needs met, but because they were not held they didn't grow and some died? Children are not going to say, "Dad, you working late every night has made me feel insecure. Would you please give me a hug and let me ramble about what happened at school today?" Or "Mom, my teacher didn't let me have a very long drink at the water fountain, and then Sandra kept ignoring me and playing with Barbra, so I need you to show me how important I am to you." No, they will be clingy, whiny, or pick a fight with a sibling, because they think you like that one better. If the behavior is motivated out of a need for you, it does not matter how clever your consequences, they will keep misbehaving. There is a saying amongst teachers: "The child that is the hardest to love, is needing the love the most." If you are a normal parent, there will be times when you may not enjoy your child. But love is a choice, not an emotion, and it is reflected in your actions.

    One of the best practices I started was checking in with each child before I started supper. I would touch those in the house and ask them a silly question before cooking. This three minutes of undivided attention drastically eliminated my trying to cook while I had a child holding onto my leg or tattling.

Try one of these twenty discipline techniques.

16. **Setting your expectation** (every age) is communicating exactly what you want. This approach is most often used for public occasions. "When we go to the doctor's office, I want you to sit in the chairs, look at your books, and talk in a whisper. You will not run, skip, jump, or shout." The second part of this procedure is equally critical; you do not tolerate noncompliance. When she fails to comply with your previously stated expectation, the result needs to be painfully memorable.

    When she interrupts your business phone call, you excuse yourself and isolate her, then return to your call. It will be more effective and less distracting if you deal with the misbehavior immediately. This is defiance and must be dealt with quickly to deter her from ignoring your expectations.

17. **"Yes, when"** (every age) is saying yes rather than no to her request. "Yes, Polly can come over when your room passes inspection." "Yes, you will be able to go to bed later every night when I see you are sitting by the door ready for school by 7:45 every day for two weeks." "Yes, I would love to drive you over to Mark's house, but I can't because the dishwasher has to be unloaded, and the groceries, and laundry have to be put away."

18. **"Good luck with that"** (every age) is responding to the child's problem without lecturing. Use this phrase instead of the tempting "I told you so". If you talk too much, she will start resenting you, rather than being annoyed with herself. "You waited to start the project until now, well, good luck with that, I'll see you in the morning." "You can't go on the field trip because you spent the money on candy? Bummer." "You expect me to me to drive you to the movies after you huffed up over my asking you to help your sister with her homework? Good luck with that."

19. **"No" and go** (preschool and younger children) is answering, "No" and leaving the temptation. I didn't teach this technique until I saw internet videos. It seems like something everyone would do. When he asks for a toy at the store say, "No", and leave the toy section. Do not

say no if you are willing to negotiate. It is okay not to give a reason as to why the answer is no. Do you think that if you say, "No, it will spoil your supper"? She is going to say, "Oh, good thinking Dad, it would spoil my appetite"? Instead she will see the explanation as the weak link to exploit, so give none.

"All you need to say is simply 'Yes' or 'No'; anything beyond this comes from the evil one" (Matthew 5:37 NIV)

If this is a change in the way you operate, you will need to use another option as well. You may need to add removal of a privilege. Examples: "If you ask again for the happy meal, your sister will play on the slide, and you will sit with me." You can use a natural consequence, "I said no to that shirt; if you fuss about it, then I will not be buying you a shirt at all."

I knew my daughter understood my "no" the day I overheard my daughter say to her friend: "My mom said not this time."

Her friend said, "I'll go ask her."

"No you can't do that, if you do, I will get in trouble."

"But if I ask…" her friend persisted.

I stepped out of the laundry room, "The answer would still be no and I might be slower to say yes next time you wanted to come over."

20. **Humor** (with every age) is distracting or removing tension, allowing the child time to make a better choice. Anytime you can diffuse a power struggle and change perspective with humor, everyone wins. For example, one child may try to boss the other one and conflict will arise. Out of desperation, one family started the "I am the boss of the family game". When a conflict over control developed, a parent would say, "Hey, I am the boss of this family and I say everyone stick out their tongue and pull their ears." The parent suggested a ridiculous rule and the entire family had to do it, even the other parent. It was like an impromptu "Simon says". Usually the silliness removed the tension and life continued.

Try one of these twenty discipline techniques.

THESE ARE NOT DISCIPLINE TECHNIQUES:

1. **Humiliation and ridicule**: Homes are meant to be a place of safety. Unconditional love and acceptance is the key to spiritual and emotional development. Please do not post on Facebook anything unflattering about your family. Do not repeat the stories of your child's misbehavior in front of your child to anyone besides your spouse. How would you feel if your wife called your boss to report your every mistake? Treat your children with the same kindness you expect from others.
2. **Yelling:** If raised voices are common in your home, Discipline Technique #5: Shouting No will not be an option. If you have an anger issue, demonstrate humility and bravery by getting professional help. Neither you, nor the ones you love, have to suffer because of this problem. Help is available.
3. **Threats:** Meaningless threats make it very difficult for a child to recognize a real consequence. Making threats and only occasionally following through with them sabotages all of your correction and makes you into a liar.
4. **Blaming:** "You're going to make me late for work." You are training her not to take responsibility. This attempt at causing guilt seldom reaps a behavior change. Instead, "I am going to be late. Obviously, you did not go to bed early enough last night. If you had, then you would not be so slow to get ready; therefore, you will go to bed thirty minutes earlier tonight. "
5. **Refusing to talk**: Thinking before you speak is wisdom, but the silent treatment is abuse.
6. **Withdrawal of love or affection**: If you fall into this habit, seek spiritual counsel. God wants to love you and heal you.
7. **Refusing to listen to reason**: Ephesians 6:4 commands parents not to provoke their child. Refusing to listen to your child's point of view is rude and provoking. If your child is presenting their ideas with respect, it is your duty to give them thoughtful consideration.

I know, some of these techniques seem to contradict one another. Parenting is an experiment; you are not going to get it right much of the time. Be a role model of integrity. When you blow it, admit it. When you struggle, pray out loud. When you succeed, dance. Often you will need to combine methodologies, but don't give up. Raising a responsible adult is too important to surrender. Yes, it is exhausting at times, but you can do hard things.

7

Use multiple discipline techniques at the same time.

1. Your ten-year-old Bryan complains, "Mom, Jill is bugging me. I asked her to leave my room and she won't." Respond, "Thank you for coming and telling me. I appreciate you didn't yell. Go and play I'll take care of Jill." (Reinforcement.) You ask Jill to come to you, because you know she is behind the door listening. You pull Jill into your lap and just hold her. (Meet emotional needs.) Once she pulls away ask, "Well, Jill, what else can you do besides bother your brother?" (Redirection.)

2. Your three-year-old Jeff keeps trying to join his older brother playing with Legos. Grab Jeff's shoulder hard enough to get his attention (firm touch) say, "No, you may play with the Duplos or your farm." (Redirection.) If he tries again, then walk him into another room without any toys. (Isolation.) "You will stay here until you decide to leave the Legos alone." After 5 minutes of quiet, ask, "Are you ready to play something in the family room? What do you choose?"

    Jeff leaves his cars the moment your head is turned. This time you take him to your room. "Jeff, do you know why I am going to spank you?" Sobbing he responds, "Cause I won't leave the Legos alone." "That is right, I expect you to obey me." Even though he is already crying, you swat him three times on the behind with your paddle. (Spanking.) You hold him saying, "You are not in trouble anymore. When you are ready to play cars or Duplos come back in the room." ten minutes later, you check on him and he is asleep. (Physical need.)

Was it the nap, or the spanking? You are not sure, but Jeff is back to normal the rest of the day.

3. You overhear Teri shout, "I hate you, Meri." Meri is on top of Teri, trying to land a punch. You shout, "No (Shouting no.) go to time-out." Meri knows that for her it means sit by the hall closet and Teri knows to sit by the laundry room where they can't see each other. (Time-out.) You ignore them until they both are quite. Give each girl paper and a pen, "Write out your side of the story and a solution, you may not leave until I say so." (Consequence.) Wait until they both have a solution before reading them. If it is at all possible, use their solutions. If not, determine the most logical consequence for each girl. The punishment may be different for each girl, because they may not be equally at fault and because what chastises one might please the other one.

4. Your two boys have been arguing the entire time you ran your errands. They fought over where they sat in the car, who walked into the store first, and who got to push the shopping cart. They whined and tattled while you tried to ignore their disputes, hoping they could resolve their conflict. (Extinction.) You tried to find out what the underlying issue was that causing the bickering. (Reasoning.) But they look at you blankly, as if to say I don't know what you are talking about.

   Once they have unloaded the car, pour yourself a lemonade and sit in your lawn chair. Explain, "Guys, you need to burn off some energy. For the next fifteen minutes, you may run, jog, jump, but you may not speak to one another and you may not stop moving. (Physical need.) I am going to enjoy the book on my phone and my lemonade. If you speak to one another or stop moving I will add 5 more minutes." Enjoy your break; you deserve it.

When my kids were early elementary school age, they would say, "DUH," every time they thought the other one said something stupid. This disrespectful habit grew quickly. I knew I had to stop it, but I didn't have the energy to invest in a big consequence. So I devised a retribution; whoever said "duh"

Use multiple discipline techniques at the same time.

had to thump their nose with their thumb and middle finger. It did sting a little, and I didn't trust them to thump each other's nose, so they had to do it to themselves.

I was saying, "Flick," while driving or eating breakfast and they were flicking their own noses. This became like the game kids play, where they count Volkswagen Beatles. They tried to catch one another saying duh, so that the other one had to thump their nose. Changing the competition was incredibly effective. The flick was not the deterrent; they didn't want the other one to catch them saying duh.

Persistence is important when disciplining your children. Even when they want to be good, they are going to struggle. You are going to blow it as well. But keep at it; fruit will come. Ask God for help.

"I don't understand myself at all, for I really want to do what is right, but I can't. I do what I don't want to—what I hate. I know perfectly well that what I am doing is wrong, and my bad conscience proves that I agree with these laws I am breaking." (Romans 8:15,16 TLB)

Part 2: Relational Parenting and Successful Procedures

8

Relational parenting prioritizes the child's long term benefit.

Relational parenting is not for the parents who want to be their child's best friend or those who smother their children with attention. It means that the parents work at knowing their child intimately with the same dedication they use in reinforcing the boundaries. They consider each child's unique personality when setting expectations and enforcing limits.

RELATIONAL PARENTS SUFFER FROM THE CONSEQUENCES ALONG WITH THEIR CHILDREN. Something dramatic like taking a bullet for our children may be easier than suffering with them the consequences of their mistakes. However, it is our job to put the character development of our children ahead of our comfort.

One example of the many sacrifices my husband and I made was the first time we tried to get away, leaving our son home alone. Before we left the county, we realized he had gone to the lake with a friend with no adult supervision. Disappointed, we came back, packed him a bag and took him with us.

Another example is when my daughter in 6th grade lost twenty dollars. We guessed it fell out of the envelope. She was selling something for school. I could have provided the twenty dollars and say "be more careful next time"; however, I had backed into a mailbox that week. I was watching, but I couldn't see it and I guessed wrong. No one came and bailed me out of my problem. I thought she was old enough to learn that I will not always be available to solve her problems. I explained, "I am really sorry; I know the frustration of losing money." By my expression, she knew I was not punishing. "I hate that unless you find the twenty-dollar bill, you will need to use your birthday money. I wish real life wasn't so hard." When dealing with a situation like this, your tone must be empathetic. If you are angry, if you are saying, "I told you to"… then you will damage your relationship. Would you want your spouse to respond with a hug or a lecture if you made a costly mistake?

RELATIONAL PARENTS PROVIDE DIFFICULTIES.

"I am here to guide you from the path of destruction. I want you to succeed, but I will step aside and let you fail. If you won't learn from my words, I will let your mistakes teach you. I love you too much to let you bomb completely, but I will do whatever I must to help you be the capable person God designed." This is always expressed in a sincere loving attitude, not with sarcasm.

Example: "How can I help you remember that you must brush your teeth before bed? I tried the note on the pillow, I tried giving you a check on the chart, and neither of those helped. Unless you can think of a better way to help you remember, I will start giving you a swat on your bottom."

Example: "How can I help you remember that the trash is carried to the curb on Mondays? I tried marking your calendar, I tried putting the trash can in the hall, but you still forgot. I think that an extra chore every day this week might make the trash more memorable. But please don't worry, I won't make you remember the extra chores. I will remind you by not allowing any media until the extra chore is completed. Today I would like all the windows cleaned. I am keeping my fingers crossed this chore idea works; if you forget next week I am not sure what I will try to help you remember."

RELATIONAL PARENTS KEEP RESPONSIBILITY, FREEDOM AND EGO IN PROPORTION.

These parents have enough self-control to deny themselves of something they want, if it benefits their child. When their son needs help with homework, a spanking, or a hug, they will lay down their phone, turn off the TV and give him their undivided attention. They will also say, "No, you have had enough sugar, media, or time with friends." "I will not take you to Wal-Mart, I am resting." "Sorry, but you left your book at school, so you will have to experience the consequences."

They also make financial or emotional sacrifices so their children can gain experience. For example: We allowed our teenage children to fly with their high school band to Pearl Harbor two months after the 911 attack. When we first agreed to this trip, the financial burden was the biggest concern. (Hawaii is still an unrealized dream for my husband and I.) You can imagine our emotional and spiritual struggle, trusting God to keep them safe. We chose to ignore our fears and allow our children to participate.

When a butterfly comes out of her cocoon, she must struggle or she will not be able to fly. If a person assists the escape by making the opening bigger, the insect will be earth-bound. If you prevent disappointment, boredom, painful consequences, learning through mistakes, and protect her from people who challenge her, she will be handicapped emotionally, spiritually, and socially. She needs to experiment, testing her skills to see what she enjoys and where her talents are strongest. If you tell her everything she does is wonderful, or protect her from failure, she will not have an honest understanding of herself. She will only know what you think.

Ninety years ago moms did not spend weeks theming their children's birthday parties, bedrooms, or social gatherings. Dads didn't work extra hours in their jobs so that their children could wear clothes and shoes of specific brands. Those children are now called "the greatest generation." Occasionally we need to stop and ask ourselves, is this for me, to impress my friends, or because it is a special treat for my son?

RELATIONAL PARENTS DO NOT TRY TO LIVE VICARIOUSLY THROUGH THEIR CHILDREN.

When your baby is born, you are her whole life and she becomes yours. You are responsible to meet her every need. In the beginning every toddler needs an audience oohing and clapping. Eventually it is inappropriate to cheer with each step she takes, each letter she writes, and each somersault she does. When a parent tries to be involved in every moment of his or her child's life, an unhealthy attachment occurs. She will become dependent on constant feedback.

Too insecure to work independently, Frank leaves his seat half way through every assignment. He must have verification before he continues. When Mrs. Thompson comments on Sally's paper, he immediately wonders what is wrong with mine. You are raising a future adult who needs to stop looking for validation from others.

Parents too immersed in their son's life say: "You were robbed, you were the best, that (coach, teacher, judge) needs to be replaced." Subliminally the parent is saying, "You are too fragile to handle any disappointment." This handicaps him from learning from failures. He interprets their words to mean: I can't love you if you aren't perfect; therefore, you are perfect and everyone else is wrong.

Children who are "people pleasers" and "codependent" will not take responsibility for their own emotions. Often they are incapable of making a decision, crippled from the fear of failure. They will be less likely to try something new, fearing they will let their parents down. They believe their parent's love is contingent on their being the most wonderful perfect son or daughter.

When parents don't hover, their son will take more chances. He knows that mom and dad love him the same amount regardless of his successes or failures. If he tries and doesn't succeed, he'll hear, "You were brave to try. What will you do differently next time?" Feeling encouraged, he faces life's challenges, honestly and with hope.

Overinvolved parents react emotionally. When minor achievements are dramatically celebrated, the major accomplishments become less meaningful. If you throw an expensive party when she turns eight, send florist flowers for valentines at ten, provide a limo ride for the first day of 6th grade, give her pearls at fourteen and a car at sixteen, what is left to make prom or graduation special? Anticipation increases joy. These inflated revelries create children less satisfied with themselves, others, and life. Practice until you can sincerely say, "I am sorry, but life is not all about you. "

RELATIONAL PARENTS ACCEPT THEIR CHILD'S EMOTIONS.

Let your child be disappointed; do not give false esteem. Avoid over-praising your child, by saying things like, "You are the best kid in the whole world."

Relational parenting prioritizes the child's long term benefit.

"I know that you can do anything if you try hard enough." Don't lie to your daughter; she has her limits. Do not give your son credit for the things he can't control. Example: "I am so proud of you for being so tall." Rather say, "I am so glad you are the boy God selected for me. I am honored to watch how you are becoming less selfish."

Choose to emphasize the satisfaction he is feeling, instead of focusing on pleasing others. "I see that today yellow is your favorite color." Not, "I like the yellow picture." Encourage by saying, "Although you don't think it is fun to go to Aunt Margaret's; you can still decide to have a good attitude and not be miserable," rather than saying, "Please make everyone happy by acting cheerful at Aunt Margaret's."

Emotionally strong parents inspire their children. This is different from praising them. Only God is worthy of praise. His very character and nature stirs worship in my heart. Exaltation is scary. Children cannot live up to adulation. When parents worship their children, they are creating idols. Being an idol is too much pressure on anyone. Children need optimism with guidance for success.

Be descriptive and empower your daughter to reach to her goal. For example: "You were kind when you gave your toy to Sharon." Or, "It is okay that you didn't get a 100% on your spelling; I know you practiced out loud and in writing. I don't get everything correct all the time either." Or, "I think being in track is a great stress reliever for you. I see how much you love running." "You are showing me that you are growing up. Last year when I would say it is time to go home you cried; today you said, 'okay' even though you didn't want to leave."

Do not fear her wrath; model using a soft answer to calm anger. She may attempt to manipulate your resolve through fury or self-pity. Hold firm, she needs stability from you. This doesn't mean you don't empathize with her. You will feel her pain: embarrassment, anger, outrage, helplessness. Just do not make it worse by adding your emotions to the mix. Demonstrate the proper way of expressing emotion. I was working with a parent of a first grader. As she shared the story of his behavior, she started to cry. He hugged her repeating, "It will be okay Momma." Once he left the room, I addressed the inappropriate role reversal. He was parenting her. It is too much pressure for a six-year-old to be responsible for a hormonal forty-year-old woman. Action, not emotion, is our methodology.

RELATIONAL PARENTS PUT THEIR CHILD'S MATURITY OVER THEIR OWN COMFORT.

"I am here to give you the skills you need for best possible life." Never make a threat, or list a result that you will not follow through. By always being honest, your son knows all the facts when making a decision.

Example: In 6th grade my son started getting lazy about paying attention and doing assignments in school. I had tried several consequences to "help him remember" what was expected of him. "I can only think of one more way to assist you with school and that is to spend the day with you in class. Obviously, once you get to school you forget everything, but if I sat beside you, you would have me as a reminder. I could carry a folding chair. I would enjoy meeting all the kids in your class. I did have one other idea. We could print off a picture of me for you to put in your notebook, that might be enough? If it is, then I wouldn't have to use a day of vacation to go to school with you. What do you think?"

Needless to say, the picture worked and I didn't go to school. He finally decided it was worth doing his assignments if it kept his mom from embarrassing him at school. This would not work with a younger child who might like you at school, or if I had not followed through on every threat so far. Yes, I absolutely would have gone to school, fortunately back then I would not have had as much red tape to go through to get permission to be in the school.

GOD IS OUR EXAMPLE.

Our Heavenly Father not only provided the commandments for his people, but He also revealed His character throughout the Bible. Jesus died so that people could have an intimate relationship with Him. God demonstrates His patience, grace, mercy, provision, and love, because He wants us to know Him just as He knows us. King David knew how much God cared about him specifically.

Relational parenting prioritizes the child's long term benefit.

> *"You have searched me, Lord, and you know me. You know when I sit and when I rise; you perceive my thoughts from afar. You discern my going out and my lying down; you are familiar with all my ways. Before a word is on my tongue you, Lord, know it completely. How precious to me are your thoughts, God! How vast is the sum of them! Were I to count them, they would outnumber the grains of sand; when I awake, I am still with you. Search me, God, and know my heart; test me and know my anxious thoughts. See if there is any offensive way in me, and lead me in the way everlasting." (Psalms 139 1-4. 17, 18, 23, 24 NIV)*

As a relational parent, God does not ignore David's sin. He enforces the standards, He maintains His authority, and He accepts us as we are. Numerous times, scripture reminds us that God punishes wickedness. This discipline is a sign of love.

> *"My son, do not make light of the Lord's discipline, and do not lose heart when he rebukes you, because the Lord disciplines the one he loves, and he chastens everyone he accepts as his son. (Hebrews 12:5, 6 NIV)*

David trusted God's judgments, because he knew God's heart. Our children are more likely to submit to our correction when they feel the security of our love. When God holds David accountable, David repents, admitting that ultimately he has sinned against God. David feels how much God values him. When children grasp their individual importance to their parents, they will not be "provoked" when corrected. Relational parents balance their need to control with their child's individual need to explore and discover who they are.

> *Fathers, don't exasperate your children by coming down hard on them.* **Take them by the hand and lead** *them in the way of the Master. (Ephesians 6:4 MSG)* (Emphasis is mine.)

> *"Fathers, **do not provoke your children to anger**, but bring them up in the discipline and instruction of the Lord. (Ephesians 6:4 ESV)* (Emphasis is mine.)

Accept that your daughter is a unique person designed by God. (See chapter 16: "Accepting Your Child's Temperament".) Give her the freedom to question your values, before she accepts them as her own. It is preferable that she experiments with her beliefs while she is living at home. By the time she goes to college, she needs to know what she believes and why. God gave her freewill, did you want to be a carbon copy of your parents? So expect her to challenge your values, be prepared to explain your priorities. If she is not interested in the same things as you are; then you expand your interests.

Raising children is a tag team sport, and the strongest parent takes over when the other is physically, mentally, or emotionally exhausted. Although parenting is a major priority in your life, you will not be a successful parent if you do not maintain a life apart from your child. If you are a single parent, it is even more critical for you to have a strong support system of friends.

Yes, childrearing is hard, but God will equip you. You can do it, but don't try to do it alone. Parenting requires great wisdom as to how to empower each child. It requires an incredible sense of balance as to being involved without taking over. Seek God's guidance as to when to let your child fail and when to intervene.

9

Chores create capable adults.

Jesus spent time training the disciples and then He gave them duties.

> *"When Jesus had called the Twelve together, he gave them power and authority to drive out all demons and to cure disease, and he sent them out to proclaim the kingdom of God and to heal the sick." (Luke 9:1,2 NIV)*

He didn't wait until He knew the disciples would do everything right before He sent them out. He let them experience failure. Their mistakes became teachable moments.

> *"Jesus replied, 'how long shall I stay with you? How long shall I put up with you? Bring the boy here to me." (Matthew 17:17 NIV)*

Even Jesus was frustrated at how slow they learned. He knew that one day the responsibilities of His Father's kingdom would rest on their shoulders, so He kept on loving, guiding, empowering, and trusting them. Remembering Jesus' example will help you parent with the end in mind. Raising children to be confident adults means teaching them to be competent in dealing with daily life challenges. These methods take more time than words, but they are effective.

When you are the first boy in your peer group getting to climb a ladder to clean out the gutters, your confidence soars. Chores develop self-reliance.

By following these steps, you will not only give your son the ability to thrive on his own, but also, you will benefit from his contribution to the household.

STEPS IN SKILL DEVELOPMENT:

1. Introduce the chore before you think he is ready to tackle it. If you wait until he can do a perfect job at the task, it will not be a fun confidence booster. There is an age-graded list provided at the end of this chapter to suggest when skills can be developed.
2. Invite him to do a specific chore with you a few times. He will love being your helper. Explain what you are doing and why you are doing the job. Emphasize the importance of the task.
3. Play "I will be your helper". Once your daughter starts to lose interest in helping you with that chore, turn the tables and you take on the role of assistant. Ask, "What should I do first?" Letting her guide, you deliberately make a mistake for her to fix.
4. Lower your standards just a bit; it is important that you do not go behind and correct her work in a noticeable way. When I returned home from surgery once, my mother-in-law had refolded all my towels, and rearranged my dresser drawers. Instead of feeling the love she was showing, I felt judged as inadequate.
5. Brag to others about the good job your son does with the chore; then release that task to be his responsibility. Thank him for contributing to the family.
6. As his maturity increases, raise your expectations for his performance.

The tone of voice you use when teaching your three-year-old to make his bed is of course very different from when you are teaching your eight-year-old to wash the car, or your thirteen-year-old to mow the grass. Nevertheless, you always do the task together a few times, demonstrating and explaining, before you expect him to work independently. Think of your home as a laboratory where your daughter develops the expertise she will need when on her own.

Chores create capable adults.

By letting her experiment and learn from her small mistakes while you are nearby she will avoid making larger more serious errors. Notice how her abilities progress to tasks that are more difficult.

SUGGESTIONS OF RESPONSIBILITIES BY AGE RANGE
2 to 3-year-olds can:

1. Put away toys. A few specific toys in specific locations. Do NOT say, "Go pick up all the toys"; that is completely overwhelming.
2. Use a hand-held vacuum that is battery charged.
3. Make her bed.
4. Set the table for a meal, making sure each person gets one of each item. This chore teaches a math concept.
5. Wipe up his spills.
6. Clear their place at the table. Put the dishes on the counter after cleaning the leftovers off the plate into the trash can.
7. Wash their hands and face.
8. Dress themselves in clothes with elastic.
9. Place boxed or canned goods from the grocery sacks on a lower shelf.
10. Carry waste paper baskets.

4-year-olds can:

1. Give pets a scoop of food and pour a cup of water into their bowl.
2. Water plants with a water hose.
3. Dust the furniture.
4. Spread butter on sandwiches.
5. Prepare cold cereal.
6. Cut fruit with a plastic knife.
7. Hold the hand mixer.
8. Get the mail and newspaper.
9. Fold towels and wash cloths.
10. Match socks.

5-year-olds can:

1. Vacuum the floors.
2. Supervise younger sibling when parent is outside.
3. Make their own sandwich or simple breakfast and clean-up afterwards.
4. Prepare salad by tearing lettuce, slicing tomatoes, and cucumbers, but not carrots or onions.
5. Hang their clothes in the closet, fold, and put clothes in their drawers.
6. Clean mirrors and windows.
7. Separate clothing for washing, putting white clothes in one pile and colored in another.
8. Pull weeds.
9. Help clean out the car.
10. Use microwave.
11. Take out the garbage.
12. Check to make sure their backpack has everything each night using a pictured check list.
13. Order their own food at a restaurant after discussing their selection with you. It is important they learn to speak to strangers in business settings.

6 to 8-year-olds can:

1. Bake by following a recipe on a boxed mix.
2. Brown ground beef.
3. Use can opener and dishwasher.
4. Make grocery list.
5. Clip coupons.
6. Run washer and dryer.
7. Take care of a garden.

Chores create capable adults.

8. Help younger children with chores and homework.
9. Wash car.
10. Make small purchases.
11. Sweep and mop floors.
12. Wrap gifts.

9 to 12-year-olds:

1. Pack their own suitcase.
2. Bathe dog.
3. Cook complete meals.
4. Mow the grass.
5. Clean out gutters.
6. Rake and bag leaves.
7. Clean the entire bathroom.
8. Ride bike to purchase groceries.
9. Set alarm and get ready for school without supervision.
10. Iron shirts.

13 to 15-year-olds

1. Make online purchases.
2. Balance checkbook and credit card statements.
3. Supervise siblings in quarterly deep clean of the house inside and out.
4. Complete all holiday decorating.
5. Plan and supervise younger sibling's birthday party.
6. Find employment in babysitting, lawn care, or house cleaning.
7. Make minor household repairs.
8. Paint home.
9. Maintain the family appointment calendar.

16 to 18-yearolds

1. Buy family groceries.
2. Maintain family and personal automobile.
3. Buy their own clothing.

"A person can do nothing better than to eat and drink and find satisfaction in their own toil. This too, I see, is from the hand of God," (Ecclesiastes 2:24 NIV)

10

Meal time as an example of parenting with respect.

Every relationship will occasionally experience a battle of wills. From eliminating the pacifier to establishing a curfew, from potty training to choosing friends, parents and children will clash. Convincing their child to eat is frustrating for most parents. So I chose it as the example of respectful priority-driven parenting.

Every day nutritionist, doctors, and weight loss gurus contradict one another as to the healthiest diet. Humans have so many emotions attached to specific foods, and so many rituals concerning meals; it is understandable why parents struggle in this area. At the risk of sounding like a food guru, I will try to provide you with a guilt-free common sense approach to getting your child to eat what you want.

MAKE SURE YOU ARE LOGICAL, NOT EMOTIONAL.

Do not nag your son about the amount he eats. When a toddler turns two, his or her body growth slows down and so do appetites. There will be days when he will hardly eat at all and days when he will want to snack constantly. Watch portion size; it overwhelms him to have too much food and if his foods touch.

He can fill up on the beverages and then not want food, so limit the amount of juice and milk he drinks. Children are not designed to eat only three meals a day, so offer healthy snacks. If you are serving only nutritious options, he will choose healthy things.

> **Jr. won't taste the meatloaf. What are your options?**
>
> **1.** Let him dip it in ketchup or ranch dressing?
>
> **2.** Bribe him with another food to taste it.
>
> **3.** Say, "You can't leave the table until you taste it."
>
> **4.** Ignore him if he makes a face or complains.
>
> **5.** Say, "Way to be brave," when he takes a bite.
>
> **6.** Pretend not to notice when he slips it to the dog.
>
> **7.** Say, "If you don't want the meat loaf, you can make a peanut butter sandwich. But I am not cooking anything until breakfast."
>
> **Which option reflects your values? Which option will best create a confident healthy adult?**

Mgs, where they only want one thing to eat for weeks at a time. So decide if you really care that he will only consume peanut butter or mac and cheese for lunch for the next three months. If the answer is yes, I do care, then do not ask him what he wants for lunch. Simply say, "Today we are having…" Do not let him know that he ever had an option. If your answer is no, it's not a big deal that he is in a jag. Then ask your pediatrician about adding a vitamin.

TEACH HER TO LISTEN TO HER BODY.

When she says that she isn't hungry, don't make her eat. Millions of us with weight problems can no longer tell if we are hungry, or when we are full, because to please our parents we ate whenever, and as much as they put on our plates. We are struggling to change our programing. Many children will not eat when holidays, company, and location overstimulate them. They will make up the missed meal later. Make the quantity a non-issue. Serve a healthy variety of foods and assume your kids will eat them.

Do not make a big deal about her preferences. Respect her enough to let her say, "I prefer carrots over broccoli." How would you feel if people made you eat something you do not like? No food is worth the hostility created when she is forced to eat broccoli. I am not saying always cook carrots and never cook broccoli. But it is unrealistic to think she will eat everything at every meal.

Without emotion say, "I expect you to eat either salad, or green beans. Which would you like?" If you eat a variety of cooked and raw vegetables, she will be more willing. If you turn meals into power struggles, everyone's digestion suffers. You can force peas into her mouth, you might force her to swallow, but you can't force her to keep the peas down. When my husband was a child his mother forced his friend to eat a vegetable she cooked. He threw up. Find a way to hide vegetables into the foods she prefers.

LET THE NATURAL CONSEQUENCES, NOT YOUR EMOTIONS, BE THE TEACHER.

Most adults are not forced to consume foods we hate; however, most of us do occasionally have to eat something we don't enjoy. You are preparing your son for adulthood, so in the instances the meals are not what he prefers, do not cook him anything different. Only occasionally cater a meal to please the picky eater, even if your spouse is the finicky one, this gives the picky eater too much power and attention.

Do not praise your child for eating everything. I was the star in my family, I ate to get my mother's approval. Since it made Moma happy for me to devour my vegetables, I ate a whole lot of everything to make Moma really happy. My younger sister went the other way, mother worried, fretted and gave her special meals; because she was picky. Do not let your children manipulate you; instead prepare a nutritious variety.

When your daughter wants a snack say, "You may have: raisins, an apple, a slice of bread, a chunk of cheese, raw almonds, peanut butter, or yogurt; be sure to clean-up after yourself." If she is really hungry, and not eating out of boredom, she will choose something healthy. If she is bored, there is not enough food in your house to satisfy her.

One of my friends with four children cooks a family sit-down meal most nights. Seldom is it everyone's favorite. Their mantra is, "If you don't like it, there is always peanut butter. If you don't want peanut butter, then it never hurts to miss a meal." There is no shame or cajoling. It is very matter-of-fact, tonight mom made tacos, beans, and salad; you may take it or leave it. Whether each child eats or not she or he is expected to sit at the table with everyone. (No one brings their cell phone to the table either.)

Food is not a bribe, punishment or for comfort. If you use desert for a reward for good eating, you are teaching your son to eat so he can get sugar. Sugar is addictive, so use it in moderation, if it is forbidden it becomes more enticing. Parents say, "If I didn't use bribery and threats, my child would starve." If this is true, their child needs professional help; because his refusing to eat is a sign of a much bigger emotional and behavioral problem. Help him to reduce his sugar intake by giving him water to drink.

The bottom line is: Why make meals a power struggle? Let the natural consequence of hunger be the teacher. Choose to make meals pleasant, and not a daily battle, by not making any food or meal overly important.

11

Autopsy your parenting failures to discover warning signs.

Learning how to autopsy your successes and failures is a critical skill for self-improvement. Recognizing the benefit of self-evaluation, realizing when further examination is needed, and working through the process requires perseverance and self-awareness.

> *Search me, God, and know my heart; test me and know my anxious thoughts. See if there is any offensive way in me, and lead me in the way everlasting. (Psalms 139: 23,24 NIV)*

A HYPOTHETICAL EXAMPLE:
The event: your daughter comes home thirty minutes past curfew. You explode: "I have had it with your disrespectful attitude! You are grounded for a month." You refuse to listen to her excuses and she responds softly "OK". Her soft response jars you into realizing that you were overreacting. Had she yelled back, you wouldn't have immediately realized you were out of control emotionally. When your reactions are out of sync with the circumstances, follow these steps.

STEP 1. LIST WHAT HAPPENED JUST BEFORE YOUR BIG MISTAKE OR BIG SUCCESS.
Fifteen minutes is often far enough back to investigate; however, the contributing circumstances for this example go back a few days before. Example list of events:

   a. I have not been able to sleep lately because of the tension from work.
   b. I have been lax about discipline; my mind is on work.

c. My daughter went to the football game after party without her phone. I discovered her phone on the hall table when I called to set her curfew.
d. She ALWAYS forgets something: her phone, her money, her permission slip, etc.
e. She left before I got home from work, so I didn't have an opportunity to talk about curfew.
f. She was thirty minutes later than her normal curfew.

STEP 2. LIST EVERYTHING YOU WERE FEELING BEFORE, DURING, AND RIGHT AFTER.

Emotions act like the warning lights on the dashboard of your car. They alert you to a problem. Emotions are chemical reactions; they are not sinful. Feelings can be controlled, but the point of step 2 is not to judge your feelings, instead acknowledge them. Be descriptive.

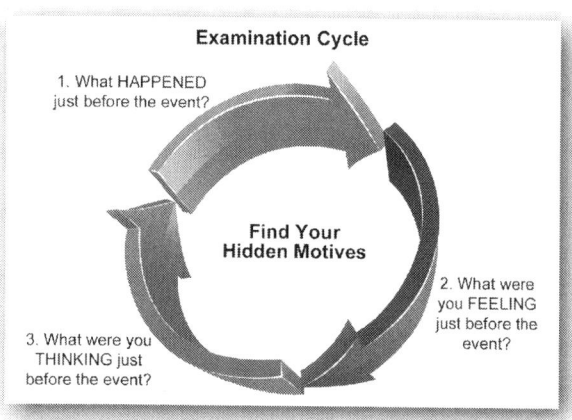

- I was physically **exhausted** and **frustrated** that she was keeping me from bed.
- I felt **angry** that she forgot her phone and wasn't home yet.
- I felt **unappreciated** by my family and my job.
- My **self-pity** was joined to **indignation**.
- I felt **helpless** and **useless** at not being able to contact her.
- There was **guilt** and **disappointment** for not getting home earlier.
- I was **scared** that she could be hurt.
- I was **embarrassed** that I wasn't sure what time the party would be over, making me feel **like a bad** parent.

Autopsy your parenting failures to discover warning signs.

STEP 3. LIST EVERYTHING YOU WERE THINKING MINUTES BEFORE.

Your self-talk is the most important information in this process. List the places your mind wandered just before the event even if it had nothing to do with the topic. Read what you wrote in steps 1 and 2 if necessary to remember what you were believing at the time. You may have reacted to those thoughts, even though they were incidental. Although I listed the thoughts in outline form for readability, write whatever comes to mind even if it is just phrases. We will examine the power of controlling our thoughts later.

a. She is just like everyone else, taking advantage of my good nature. Treating me like my ideas do not matter.

b. My mother warned me about nights like these, she said I would pay for all the times I deliberately ignored curfew.

c. If she cared about this family, she would set a better example, she is so selfish, she doesn't care that I am losing sleep and am worried about her, while she is off laughing without a care in the world.

d. There is no excuse for her delay; I will not even give her a chance to explain. If I did, I might soften, and this time I have to stay tough. I have been too easy on these kids. I noticed her sister hasn't cleaned their bathroom in a week. I swear I have to stay on top of these kids or they will take advantage. Well, things are about to change.

e. What is a matter with the youth pastor keeping these kids out so late? I am tempted to call someone else to see if their kids are home yet. I wish I knew if she was sitting at Sonic Drive-In. I'll give her fifteen more minutes, then I am calling around. I don't care if it embarrasses her.

f. I am such a lousy parent; I bet the Fergusons never have this problem. I should have gotten home sooner; I should have paid better attention to what she said. I keep meaning to download that family app that helps with keeping track of everyone's schedule.

If your goal was to learn from a successful event, you can stop here. Read over the self-talk and notice what you said to give you the ability to react appropriately to your circumstance. However, if you are hoping to learn from a mistake, reverse the cycle.

2ND PART OF THIS PROCESS IS TO TAKE EACH THOUGHT AND CHANGE IT TO REFLECT THE TRUTH. IF YOU ARE OBSERVANT, YOU WILL SEE WHERE SATAN HAS DECEIVED YOU.

> *"We demolish arguments and every pretension that sets itself up against the knowledge of God, and we take captive every thought to make it obedient to Christ." (2 Corinthians 10:5 NIV)*

> *"Finally, brothers and sisters, whatever is true, whatever is noble, whatever is right, whatever is pure, whatever is lovely, whatever is admirable—if anything is excellent or praiseworthy—think about such things." (Philippians 4:8 NIV)*

STEP A. REWRITE EACH THOUGHT WITH THE TRUTH BASED ON OBJECTIVITY AND SCRIPTURE.

Pay attention to which thoughts cause fear, self-pity, hopelessness, and shame. By monitoring your thoughts, you will discover unrealistic expectations, irrelevance, and lies from satan. In this fictional example, I took what I wrote in step 3 and rewrote it focusing the facts instead of feelings. If you are still too emotional to think rationally, wait and try again later.

a. She is not out to hurt me. She is a typical teen. She is more courteous than most. I am not going to blame her for the tension I feel at work.
b. Just because I took advantage of my curfew, doesn't mean my daughter is taking advantage. I believe in *treating everyone the way I want to be treated*. I will give her the benefit of the doubt. I will listen to her explanation and then I will decide the best action to take.
c. She does care about her family. I saw her helping her brother with his homework. She is not trying to make anyone miserable. Concentrate on appropriate consequences for her missing curfew; do not plot revenge.

Autopsy your parenting failures to discover warning signs.

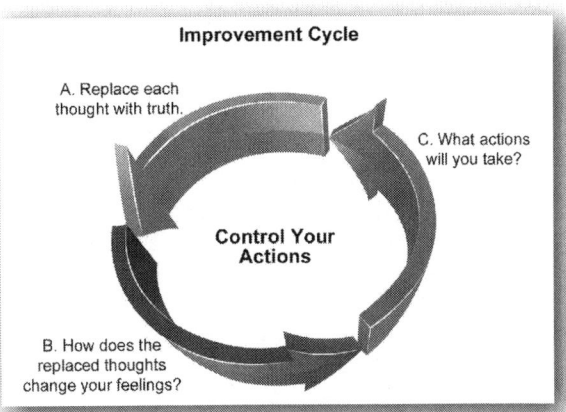

d. I will deal with her sister's not cleaning the bathroom by letting her clean my bathroom as well. I have not been diligent to enforce expectations. I will discipline each child individually, not as a group.

e. Perhaps I need to volunteer to help with the snacks for one of these after football game parties, so that I will know what is happening. If she did go to Sonic, I need to increase her penalty.

f. If I am forced to call around looking for her, I will be calm, I will be rational, I will remember my priority is her safety at this moment.

g. I am a normal parent. No one is going to do everything right all the time. God didn't place my children in the Ferguson's home. He will help me. I am going to make a better effort to pay attention to the children and I will download the family schedule app now.

STEP B. REWRITE EACH FEELING NOW THAT YOU ARE THINKING MORE CLEARLY.

How do the replaced thoughts change your feelings? What are your dominate feelings? How intense is your emotion?

a. I feel love, compassion, and acceptance toward my daughter.
b. I am determined to be reasonable as I punish her for breaking curfew.
c. I feel calmer and more in control of myself and the environment.
d. I am not as critical of the youth minister.
e. I don't feel shame and embarrassment about my parenting performance; I don't feel as angry toward my daughter.

STEP C. DECIDE WHAT ACTIONS YOU WILL TAKE AND ACKNOWLEDGE THAT SOME CIRCUMSTANCES CANNOT BE CHANGED.

Do what you can and accept the fact that some things you are powerless to change. As you improve what you can, the other items will become less important.

a. I will do more to make sure my work stays at work.
b. I will regain control of my home by enforcing all rules.
c. I will set an alarm for 9:15 each night to remind me to make sure each one knows he or she is loved.
d. I will explain what she is to do if the church activity is not over before curfew.
e. If she had taken her phone, the curfew would not have been such a big issue. My first priority is teaching her to take her phone with her. If she did not come straight home afterwards, I will give her an earlier curfew next time.

Use this system to analyze a disagreement with someone, a recurring sin, or any behavior you want to change. Change your thinking, follow your action plan, and your success will make you so happy that you will continue the process. With practice, you will feel the warning signals of overreaction or under-reaction telling you to change your thinking. As you examine your thoughts, you will discover faulty beliefs. When you make a conscious effort to believe the truth, your emotions and reactions will become more appropriate. This is what is described below.

"Do not conform to the pattern of this world, but be transformed by the renewing of your mind. Then you will be able to test and approve what God's will is—his good, pleasing and perfect will." (Romans 8:2 NIV)

12

Accept your child as made by God.

When you learn to recognize your child's God-given temperament as a blessing, you will have a better relationship with your child. Accepting your child as she or he is is a key aspect of unconditional love. Your child is God's unique creation, He personally designed his or her disposition.

> *"The word of the LORD came to me, saying, "Before I formed you in the womb I knew you, before you were born I set you apart; I appointed you as a prophet to the nations." (Jeremiah 1:4, 5 NIV)*

Each person is born with his or her own quirky personality. Trying to make your child go against her nature is like trying to make a fish fly, frustrating everyone. Satan tries to misguide parents into focusing on temperaments causing them to overlook the true disobedience.

Visualize each of these characteristics on a continuum between 1-10. If your child is a 1, 2, 9 or 10, he will need skills for specific occasions. He may need to use self-restraint to follow social etiquette. However, never try to change your child's temperament. When the temptation arises read Genesis 25, 26. Do not make the tragic mistakes of selecting a favorite like Isaac and Rebekah did.

ACTIVITY LEVEL

This has nothing to do with hyperactivity. Some children are born with extra energy. Even in the womb some babies are more active. This does not mean he will never be able to sit still in church, or school, but it does mean that he will be happier if you bring him a book to enjoy while waiting at the table in a restaurant.

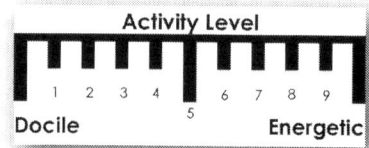

A parent can say, "Why don't you go play outside like your sister?" to the less active kid. Physical activity is important, but are you motivated by, "Why can't you be like them?" Children who are compared unfavorably to others become resentful and jealous. It will be harder for them to know you love them if you seem to suggest another person is better. The simplest solution to activating the docile child or slowing down the energetic one is for you to also participate in the activity you are suggesting.

"But in fact God has placed the parts in the body, every one of them, just as he wanted them to be." (1 Corinthians 12:18 NIV)

RHYTHMICITY AND ADAPTABILITY

Rhythmicity explains how much of a routine someone needs. Some infants come into this world eating every four hours, pooping one hour after being fed, and sleeping for several hours at a time. Other babies seem to change their patterns as soon as one seems to develop.

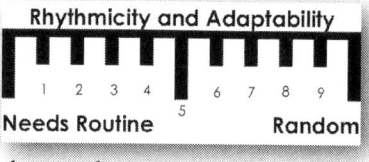

Biorhythms are also part of this category. This includes how much the time of day affects a person, i.e. night owl or early bird.

Most children thrive with regular meal times and bed times, yet a few NEED a regular routine. Without predictability, they become irritable on family vacations or when company comes. If your son is flexible, be grateful, but give a basic structure for security. If he is not, then make sure he has a snack if he has to wait for supper, or provide a relaxing activity if a nap is not an option. Do as much as you can to keep life normal; however, do not let this become an excuse for bad conduct especially once he is six years or older. Learning to cope with irregular schedules is a life skill.

INTENSITY OF REACTION

When the character of a movie is suddenly attacked, do you jump, scream, or smile? Your involuntary response developed even before you were born. When dealing with the stresses of life do you freeze up, unable to think or move?

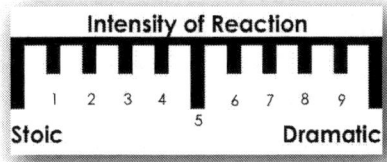

> Everyone has these traits to varying degrees. It is fascinating to see how these temperaments are very evident in some newborns. Do not confuse this with sin nature, rebellion against God. Temperaments are a portion of your child's personality.
> *"Your hands made me and formed me; give me understanding to learn your commands."*
> (Psalms 119:73 NIV)
> God gives each person the personality and talents to accomplish His specific plan.

Most of us are able to respond appropriately to life's challenges. It is not good or bad that some people are quiet when conflict arises; the Bible does encourage thinking before speaking. However, if this is so extreme that communication shuts down, then nothing is resolved. Equip your stoic daughter in how to express her feelings and ideas respectfully. Help your emotional dynamo to discern a true crisis and learn how to speak rationally. Remember neither of these temperaments is better, your job is providing the necessary abilities, so he or she can be most effective in serving God.

"The one who has knowledge uses words with restraint, and whoever has understanding is even-tempered." (Proverbs 17:27 NIV)

THRESHOLD OF RESPONSE

We receive environmental clues every moment: the smell of perfume, the furniture beyond this page, the hum of the refrigerator, and the feel of the chair. While many children ignore bruises and ear infections, others go ballistic because their clothes are scratchy. Some children will eat almost anything, while others balk at a brand change. I have a niece who was frightened of the vacuum cleaners' noise and another one that could sleep through a train whistle.

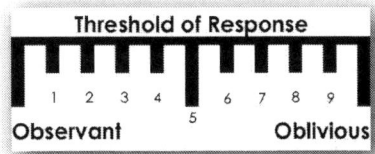

My daughter was very tender headed; no matter how carefully I brushed her hair, it still hurt. She learned to take care of her hair by first grade thus avoiding discomfort. Because my son did not complain, he suffered with an ingrown toenail for months. He had a high pain threshold. I made the mistake of thinking each of my children would communicate with me in the same way. Knowing your child's heart, motivation, and pain tolerance is critical.

REACTION TO NEW SITUATIONS

Both the overly cautious and overly confident person is self-absorbed. One extreme is a person who has never met a stranger, is curious about everything, talks over people, shares every thought that crosses his or her mind, volunteers quickly, and is ready for whatever life has around the corner. Unaware of other people, he is a tornado that blows in, leaving people stunned.

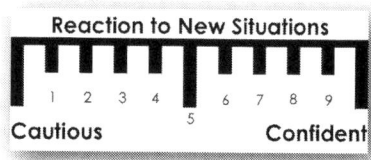

At the other end of the spectrum is the more introverted people. Dipping their toe in the swimming pool to consider if they will submerge their entire foot, they are unaware that drowning people are screaming for help right beside them. They are so concerned for their own comfort that they tune out everyone else. Shaming slow-to-warm-up children will be counterproductive when trying to make them feel secure enough to come out of their shell.

Do not let your home revolve around the extrovert; use your son's confidence to develop a servant's heart. If he turns his attention on others, he will make an impact for God. Challenge your self-conscious daughter to see others as important. When she focuses on the needs of others, she will be more confident.

> *The second is this: 'Love your neighbor as yourself.' There is no commandment greater than these. (Mark 12:31 NIV)*

Once the hesitant boy quits crying on the first day of Kindergarten, he is the perfect pupil because he will not speak unless responding to someone directly.

Wary students are happy to let their classmates shine, while they work behind the scenes. In addition, they will be less impulsive as teens.

The world also needs the risk-takers who will lead and innovate. They may cause problems, but with the right guidance, they will create ways to clean up their messes.

QUALITY OF MOOD

This is not moodiness. Moodiness, aka a bad attitude, is pouting, temper tantrums, and other manipulative behaviors. Those character issues are sin.

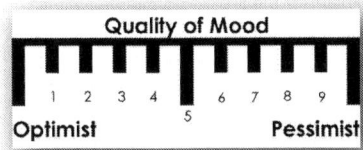

> Never label one aspect of temperament as good and another as bad. The mannerisms are only different; one trait is not morally superior to the other. It is imperative that your child feels loved and accepted as God created them. Become a student of your child, empowering his strengths and minimizing his weaknesses. For example, a wise parent will reduce the noise of television or music if her teen is easily distracted.

Everyone is either naturally more optimistic or pessimistic. Some babies are cheerful and some melancholy. Seldom do two people share the same sense of humor. Some toddlers are quicker to smile and laugh than others. You may find those giggles delightful when your daughter is three, but may annoy you when she is thirteen.

When Chris was in Kindergarten, his arm was surgically re-broken because it was not healing in the proper alignment. He said, "Well, at least I got good sleep." He was referring to the anesthesia used in his procedure. Chris is an "I won't let you rain on my parade" kid. His great outlook was a gift from birth.

However, Jeremiah was designed by God to be "the weeping prophet" (Jeremiah 1:4-7; 14:11-17). John the Baptizer was very serious. Jesus was criticized for enjoying life.

> *"For John came neither eating nor drinking, and they say, 'He has a demon.' The Son of Man came eating and drinking, and they say, 'Here*

is a glutton and a drunkard, a friend of tax collectors and sinners.' But wisdom is proved right by her deeds." (Matthew 11:18,19 NIV)

God gifted your child with either optimism or pessimism. Your task is to give them realism by letting them experience the consequences to their decisions. Your responsibility is to teach him or her not to trust in their personality, but to rely on God's power.

But he said to me, "My grace is sufficient for you, for my power is made perfect in weakness. Therefore I will boast all the more gladly about my weaknesses, so that Christ's power may rest on me." (2 Corinthians 12:9 NIV)

DISTRACTIBILITY AND ATTENTION SPAN

Is your baby a pit bull or a butterfly? Does your daughter concentrate so totally on her book that she blocks out what you are saying? Is she heartbroken if she has to go to bed before finishing her craft project? Or does she stop nursing and look at each person who enters the room?

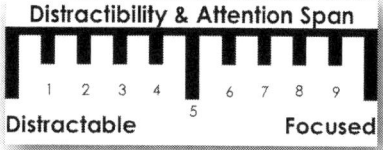

The good news is your distractible son is easily comforted. He will forget about wanting to play with the television remote when you hand him the giraffe. The bad news is he is great at starting projects, but will lose interest in finishing them. He will diligently begin straightening his room, but ten minutes into the process, he will become engrossed in playing. He is not intentionally disobeying; he just got an idea that it would look better if he lined up his action figures on another shelf.

Setting a ten-minute alarm will awaken him to get back on task. Play games requiring concentration and memorization. Include visual clues to remind him of what he must accomplish every morning before school. Absentminded children think about too many things. They may become overwhelmed and not do anything if you give too many instructions. Even as a teen, Baylor

Accept your child as made by God.

reminded his mom, "I can remember three things, if you want me to do more than that, write it down please."

> The challenge of parenting is knowing when I am disciplining because of their behavior, or my mood. Just as it is critical to have realistic expectations based on each child's age, it is imperative to recognize our own personality biases and not penalize our children for being the person God made.
> For example, if your child is an oak, do not try to make her into an apple tree.
> *"So we make it our goal to please him, (God) whether we are at home in the body or away from it."*
> (2 Corinthians 5:9 NIV)

The good news is children that focus intently think more sequentially. They tend to be logical, thinking through the steps of problem solving. They will not scatter toys like the children learning through trial and error. If it is important to them, they will work to complete the assignment to the very best of their ability. The bad news is they will throw a temper tantrum when you offer the giraffe, instead of the television remote. They can become obsessed with details, failing to see the big picture.

You may have to limit the time your son has to complete a chore. For example, "I set the alarm for five minutes, when it goes off you have to stop straightening your bed, and spend the next ten minutes vacuuming your floor." He may also need more help in making friends and socializing.

"But one thing I do: Forgetting what is behind and straining toward what is ahead, I press on toward the goal to win the prize for which God has called me heavenward in Christ Jesus. (Philippians 3:13b-14 NIV)

FRUSTRATION TOLERANCE AND PERSISTENCE

When you reconcile your bank statement, do you get it to the penny, or do you think within a dollar is close enough? Does a more difficult challenge make you more de- 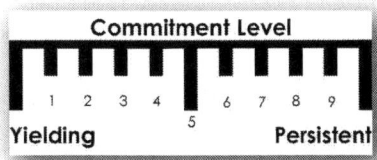 termined to succeed? How easy is it for you to throw in the towel and say, "not for me?" Do you secretly dare yourself to improve your effectiveness? I forgot how low my frustration tolerance is until I started trying to keep up with all the new technology. I felt defeated. Using the software looked so easy on YouTube, now I can't figure out what I am doing wrong. How do you feel when you get the error message?

Those who are easily frustrated may hire someone else to fix their car. They may acquiesce in a discussion over a trivial topic. They may lack the stamina or dedication needed to be a triathlete.

As with any temperament, there is a danger when taken to the extreme. People are for loving, not using, they are not obstacles to conquer. Determination can turn a hero into a villain if the goal is wrong, or the viewpoint is success at any cost.

> *"Three times I was beaten with rods, once I was pelted with stones, three times I was shipwrecked, I spent a night and a day in the open sea, I have been constantly on the move. I have been in danger from rivers, in danger from bandits, in danger from my fellow Jews, in danger from Gentiles; in danger in the city, in danger in the country, in danger at sea; and in danger from false believers. I have labored and toiled and have often gone without sleep; I have known hunger and thirst and have often gone without food; I have been cold and naked." (2 Corinthians 11:25-27 NIV)*

Paul did not allow obstacles to prevent him following God's plan for his life and at the same time he tempered his drive with humility.

> *"Do nothing out of selfish ambition or vain conceit. Rather, in humility value others above yourselves, not looking to your own interests but each of you to the interests of the others." (Philippians 2:3, 4 NIV)*

A FINAL EXAMPLE OF WORKING WITHIN YOUR CHILD'S TEMPERAMENT:

Even at ten-years-old, soft-spoken Amy, the oldest of three, had grace and dignity. Her athletic family played sports, ran, and bicycled together. Her dad, Todd, was concerned that she wasn't aggressive enough and people might take advantage of her. He cited the example, "No matter what we or the basketball coaches say, Amy will not foul anyone."

I asked, "Do her siblings take advantage of her good nature."

"Oh no she manages them just fine."

"I have never seen any kids bully her at church, is there is a problem at school?"

"No, she loves school, she participates in everything."

"Do you think you may be seeing a problem that doesn't exist?"

Once Todd accepted that Amy's temperament was a gift from God, he didn't worry so much. That was almost a decade ago; Amy excelled in everything she touched in high school. She is a star tennis player, still not aggressive, but a leader in her high school's Honor Society.

I am glad God does not let us choose our child's temperament. How would we ever decide?

Part 3- Pregnancy and The First Year

13

Parenting begins in the womb.

Mom and Dad can work together to enjoy a healthy, calm pregnancy. One of the first signs of pregnancy some women notice is that they start crying over television commercials. Hormones affect both health and emotions. Stress is more toxic with erratic hormones, so reduce your schedule, so that you can focus on your health. Emotions affect blood pressure, cause muscle aches, stomach distress, headaches and make women less likely to follow their exercise and nutrition plan. Dad, encourage mom-to-be to nap. Sleep not only restores her body, it stabilizes her mood, and improves her ability to think.

Pregnancy changes a woman's hair, teeth and nails so in addition to taking your prenatal vitamins, eat plenty of protein and nutritionally dense foods or both you and your baby will suffer. Allergies, a cold, a stress headache and hemorrhoids are all more complicated when you are pregnant. Mom's health must be a priority. Medications, alcohol, and nicotine cross the placenta. Do not assume that an item you picked up at the health food store is okay for you to take when your pregnant.

As you begin nesting, resist the temptation to buy all of the nursery gizmos and gadgets. Retailers know you want everything that will make you baby's life the best it possibly can be. There is nothing wrong with this desire, but the majority of the items will not do anything to improve the quality of your life or your baby's. In fact, overspending will increase your stress as you try to pay for it all.

For example, you will need a stroller. Do you need one that plays three kinds of music with seven reclining positions, a Global Positioning System, and a twelve-page instruction manual? Look for something lightweight, wheels that roll easily, a storage compartment for a few diapers, your wallet and keys, a cover that is adjustable to keep the sun out of the baby's eyes, straps to keep the baby in place and will fold so that it fits easily in your vehicle. If it does not come with a position to lay your baby flat on her back, then tilt the seat as far back as possible and roll a soft baby blanket then place around the sides of the baby's head for support.

Repurpose things around the house, crock pots or sauce pans of water are great to warm bottles, a soft wash cloth or hand towel is a great burp cloth, your baby will not care if his cousin's hand-me-down crib sheets are not in the same motif as his room. When you do not buy all of the "labor" saving devices, then you don't have to find places to store them or time to maintain them.

Do everything you can to make your life easier once junior comes. Freeze casseroles for you to heat up on busy days. Layer several crib sheets with your mattress protectors or rubber sheets so when there is a mess in the middle of the night you can strip the bed and not have to remake the bed. Do buy more than three sets of sheets.

Buy a strong odor resistant diaper pail, get a rocker or glider, and get a device to make white noise, or mother's heartbeat, or soft music. If scrap booking isn't your thing, or time is really hard to find, buy a calendar so that you can jot down a comment almost every day about the baby. It may help you remember things like the first tooth and it may help you to discover food allergies or other clues to fussiness if you spend thirty seconds daily documenting what is happening.

The most powerful parenting habits you can develop while the baby is still in the womb are prayer and trusting in God. Hormones make you more susceptible to worry. Start learning to do your best and trust God with the rest. It will be harder to have a consistent quiet time after the baby comes and after you return to your "normal" routine, so make it a priority now.

Start simplifying your life by removing physical clutter. Soon it will take two trips to get everything and everyone into the car unless you learn to carry less. Many of your breakables must be moved when he or she starts crawling, and you will soon find stuffed animals where your candlestick once rested.

Embrace the change, your things will be out again soon enough. The childrearing years go very fast. When you can, remove the people and activities in your life draining you emotionally. Allow parenting to change your priorities; practice saying "No, maybe I will in another season of life."

Please remember, I am not a doctor so do not substitute my opinions for the advice of professionals. I am sharing what I have learned, knowing that not all advice is appropriate for every situation.

14

Begin parenting with the end in mind now.

During his first year your son is learning whether he can trust you, and his world, this will affect his mental and spiritual health for the rest of his life. Erik Erikson called this stage "trust versus mistrust". Every time you meet his need, whether it is the need for food, a clean diaper, sleep, or security, you are teaching him that he can trust you.

Brain research is confirming things that most mothers have instinctively known. The more an infant is comforted in the early months, the more quickly he will respond to soothing in the later months. We know that neurons that are reinforced and stimulated remain in the brain while those that are not will dissolve. In simple terms, if you make him feel secure you are creating a rut of contentment in his brain. It is hard to get out of a rut. This is why babies who feel safe and secure are easier to calm.

I am not saying do not let your baby girl cry, or rush over the second she fusses. Finish making your bed or taking your shower or whatever you are doing when she wakes from her nap and starts to fuss. For the first five or six months as soon as possible, meet her needs. After that, give her the opportunity to calm herself.

We try at church to make a connection for the infant between Christian terms and the feelings of love. Teachers whisper with joy in their voice "Jesus, Bible, God, Church", and words of love as they hold a contented baby. This association makes it easier for her to trust Jesus as Lord and Savior when He tugs at her heart six to twelve years later.

Breast-feed as long as you can. In addition to the health and financial benefits, it encourages the mom to sit down and relax and just enjoy her baby. Mothers tend to feel guilty if they are doing "nothing but holding their baby". I was never one of the fortunate mothers who got her figure back simply by breast feeding, but I do believe it helped me get my strength back because when my baby needed to eat, I stopped everything, rested and drank a glass of water. I also loved that she always needed to eat right before or after supper, so my husband invariably had to finish cooking or do the dishes. Dad, there is still plenty for you to do: changing diapers, playing games, holding, bathing, dressing, singing, rocking.

After about two weeks of breast feeding, introduce an occasional bottle of breast milk. (If you do this too often, nipple confusion can occur. It takes less effort to drink from a bottle and she might stop nursing.) I did not offer my daughter a bottle until she was three months old. By waiting so late, she refused to take a bottle of anything from anyone. She also refused all food, except for saltine crackers and cheerios. So she learned to drink diluted juice from a sippy cup instead of a bottle. I weaned her at fourteen months. She went from breast to pizza.

I learned from my mistake, so I gave my son an occasional bottle after the second week. He also liked baby food. I pureed much of my food before I seasoned and froze it in ice trays, so I could zap it in the microwave, and then stir it well to make sure there were no hot spots. By nine months he was drinking well out of a sippy cup. He weaned himself without ever becoming dependent on a bottle to sleep.

You can "spoil" a baby over six months. Respond slowly to cries that are just fussy. She is old enough to play a few minutes in her crib without your removing her as soon as she awakens. Say, "No," when she wants to be held and you are vacuuming. Now is the time to start letting her learn to entertain herself occasionally.

When she starts rolling or crawling, child proof everything. God made children curious; He wants them to explore their world. Your job is to make the world as safe as possible. When necessary slap a hand, say a firm no, and remove him to another place so that he will be distracted from the dog's food.

Begin parenting with the end in mind now.

Your baby girl is not your property. As a creation of God, her life's purpose is to reflect God's glory. Over the next seventeen years your job is to transfer her dependence from you to God. Your goal is to help her discover the unique person she is then express herself within the boundaries established by God. This process begins now, not when she is potty-trained, and certainly not when she turns twelve.

15

Enjoy the first year.

I would love to give every parent the gift of knowing how to play. It is sad to see adults who have had their creativity squelched and their playful spirit destroyed. Children are a gift to be enjoyed. Their enthusiasm, smiles, and laughter give energy to life. By learning to play with your children, you will increase their intelligence and vocabulary, you will express your love in a language they can understand, and you will get insight into what they are thinking.

GAMES TO PLAY.

Smiling, talking softly, blinking your eyes are all ways to play with your newborn boy. As he begins to make sounds, mimic them. Granted, this will be a great annoyance when he mimics you at seven years of age. Nevertheless, for now this play is the precursor to conversation. By repeating the sound, you are making him aware of vocalizations and beginning to teach cause and effect. Once he is holding a small rattle, you will want to place the toy just in his reach, helping him develop the hand eye coordination needed to stomp you in a video game when he is five.

Peek-a-boo and hide the object under the blanket reinforce the concept that objects that are not seen still exist. Often when he understands this fact, he will cry for you when you are not in sight. Before he knew things were permanent, he thought you only existed when you were with him. This developmental milestone is the reason he is suddenly crying when you leave him in the church nursery.

As you lay on the floor and he pokes you in the eye, say, "eye", then point to his eye. Learning the names for things is a full time job for him and can be great fun for you. Teach "ear" by kissing it and "belly" by blowing on it.

Making him laugh will give you such joy and there are numerous ways to get a chuckle. So don't play any game that involves him hitting you and you pretending to cry. Eventually you will be trying to teach him not to hit and he will be confused, so don't play that game.

You began singing to him while he was in the womb, so don't stop now. Avoid tossing him in the air, but do bounce him on your knee and hold him out as he is flying. Encourage his crawling, the left/right alternating movement, stimulates both hemispheres of the brain.

A great game to play around seven months is build it up and let him knock it down. He will find it great fun. If you need more variety in your life, try building with plastic bowls, boxes of macaroni, or dominos. Be sure to clap enthusiastically every time he makes it fall down. This give and take is play. One word of caution, throw it off my high chair and daddy picks it up is not a fun game. Do not clap, act happy, or make the fun exclamation, "Oops". Firmly say, "No"; stop that game before it is a habit.

TOYS TO BUY

When purchasing a book, remember it needs to pass the chew test, so don't buy pop-up books or anything easily torn. In addition, look for simple illustrations, the words really do not matter, because you are going to describe the pictures. Your baby girl will not want to look at the pages in sequence. Since you will be reading this book for hours, buy one that you like. Make a photo book, placing photos of your family along with photos of her taking a bath, sleeping, reading a book. Be sure to include a photo of the family pet.

My husband and I loved teasing each other about who made the best animal sounds. Books with farm animals will entertain everyone. Keep a couple of books available anytime you leave your home. They are great when you need to amuse a child at any age. When she is older, read every book out loud before purchasing. Books with a fun rhythm will help stimulate her ears as well as her eyes.

Enjoy the first year.

Always choose toys that are not choking hazards and are easy to wipe down, because she will explore everything with her mouth. Toys that make noise when moved are fun, reinforcing the cause and affect connection. A drum set, plastic keys, and a busy box are great toys to buy. Push/pull and riding toys are great; however, a nice cardboard box will trump most store bought toys.

Do not forget about garage sales and second hand stores when looking for toys. If the toy can be thoroughly cleaned, then it is a great gift. Toddlers have no concept of new and used. If it is new to them then it is new. For the first five years of my children's lives, I often bought used items. I saved them for their birthday and Christmas gifts.

There is no reason to introduce a toddler to any technology. She will surpass your understanding of the gadgets by the time she is in 2nd grade. Focus on engaging her five senses and large muscles. Until she is at least three, there is no such thing as educational television.

If you are not sure how to play with your child, get in the floor and watch; he or she will teach you how to play. Good parents are willing to learn from their child by following their lead.

16

Parenting the first year made easier.

SLEEPING TIPS:

If baby boy fights sleep, you may try the swing, your humming and cuddling while rocking or swaying. Some babies drift off to sleep when you prop them on their side and let them cry for three or four minutes. You can also hold him tightly to your chest, blow gently into his face making him close his eyes, or lightly lay your hand over his eyes. Try yawning and taking deep breaths; yawns are contagious. Watch a YouTube video to learn how to swaddle your infant.

At about six months old he is eating a small amount of cereal and able to go for longer periods without food. This is a good time to start teaching him to sleep through the night. If he wakes because he is wet, keep everything as dark and low key as possible. Change him in the crib without turning on the overhead light. Do not talk. Reposition his blanket and whisper good night.

I made the mistake of taking my daughter back to bed with me to nurse. I could not convince her to stay in her own bed all night when she was nine months old. For three long nights I had to let her cry herself back to sleep. Though at the time it seemed like three weeks.

Another sleep challenge could have been prevented, if I had explained to our three-year-old son, "You can just roll over and go back to sleep, if you have a dream. You do not have to wake up anyone and tell them. Breakfast is the perfect time to talk about dreams."

TUMMY ACHE SOLUTIONS:

If the problem is a tummy ache, your baby girl may pull her knees into her chest, pass gas, and have pained expression on her face. If this is the case, try the football hold. In this hold, she faces down and you hold her head between your elbow and your ribs. The tummy rests in the heel of your hand while her arms and feet hang down limp. Use the heel of your hand to place pressure on the tummy. Use your free hand to pat her on the back and bottom. Often I use this while standing and swaying side to side or twisting back and forth at my waist.

Another position is to lay her face down across your lap. Put her tummy on one knee and her upper torso on the other. Lay your hand closest to her head as a stabilizer on her shoulders and back. While her arms and legs hang limply down, gently raise and lower the heel of your foot closest to the tummy. Often she will sing as you make the vibrating motion. Pat her bottom with a heartbeat rhythm. Remember you are jostling her bottom. NEVER SHAKE A BABY'S HEAD.

DRESSING YOUR INFANT MADE EASIER:

Pull shirts on by starting them on the back of the head first rather than straight down from the top. You will find this easy to do if you lay your baby down to dress him or her. Place the baby's head on the opening of the shirt then pull it forward. This will make it easier for you to protect your baby's eyes, ears, and nose as you pull the top on.

If your daughter curls her toes when you try to put on her shoes: facing her, straighten her leg and mash gently above her knee and her toes will straighten. This is a little harder to accomplish if her knees are chubby. It will save you time if you loosen the laces and approach the foot toe nail side first in a scooping motion.

GOOD PARENTS WALK AWAY.

There will be times when a baby will cry and nothing you try will work. When that happens lay your son down in his crib with his comfort item, blanket, pacifier, or toy. Then turn on soft music, turn off the light, and set your

> **"Won't quit crying!"**
> **A double-check list:**
> o Diaper?
> o Hungry or thirsty?
> o Too hot, cold or tired?
> o Mad, pained, or tired cry?
> o Check clothing including socks for rubbing?
> o Rash or insect bite?
> o Signs of fever or upset tummy?
> o Changed routine or food?

phone alarm for ten minutes. During that time, do whatever you would like to calm and comfort yourself. Get some fresh air, make a phone call, drink a glass of water, and pray. If more parents would follow this advice there would be a significant drop in child abuse.

If after ten minutes he seems to be relaxing, do not go into the room set the timer for five more minutes, and give him time to self soothe. He is just overstimulated and was sensing your tension or frustration, and so it was becoming a vicious cycle. Occasionally his emotions build and he needs to let off steam. You are not a bad parent if he is having a fretful day.

If he is still as upset, then begin the checklist again to see if you can find a reason. Continue to take deep slow breaths, and stay relaxed. If at any time you start to feel angry then place him gently back into his bed and leave the room. Document everything that happened prior to this incident. List foods he ate, and the number of dirty diapers. If you are breast-feeding, document what you ate. Use this information to find patterns. You may find it helpful to record the sound of his cry. If this continues, take your notes, and recording to see his pediatrician.

Lean on friends and family when you are exhausted or discouraged. Anyone who says this is easy is delusional or a liar. Good parents trade out with another couple, so they can have an occasional break. Life will be easier when your child can tell you what is wrong and you can sleep without interruption. There is no shame in asking for help.

A Final Word

Dear Reader,

I feel that we have a relationship that I hate to end. If you feel the same, join me on the Parenting with The End in Mind Facebook Page. Not only can we keep the conversation going, but I need your input. Which chapters would you like in my next book?

How to get out of doing your child's homework?
How to have wonderful family memories without spending big bucks?
How to foster your child's spiritual development?
How to make the most of your child's brain strengths?
Or do you have another itch I can scratch?

Stop by my blog "A Woman Trusting God". I share the lessons God is teaching me at www.jaynac.com.

Praying God's blessings for your family,
Jayna Coppedge

About the Author

Jayna Coppedge loves spending time with her two adult children. Laura and Tyler were great "guinea pigs."

Although she received a bachelor's degree with a marriage and family emphasis in 1983, she continues to study family relationships. This book is the result of the many parenting classes she has taught over the past two decades.

A children's minister for twenty-four years, she taught children of all ages, trained Sunday school teachers, and walked along with families in every life stage. Her occupation provides her with a unique perspective of family systems, observing and being in relationships with hundreds of children from birth until they leave home.

She maintains and active web presence with her blog, _A Woman Trusting God_, is a regular contributing writer for _Ask God Today_, speaks at women's conferences, and teaches weekly Bible studies and parenting classes.

Made in the USA
Columbia, SC
01 July 2017